THE TREASURES OF

·CORONATION ST.·™

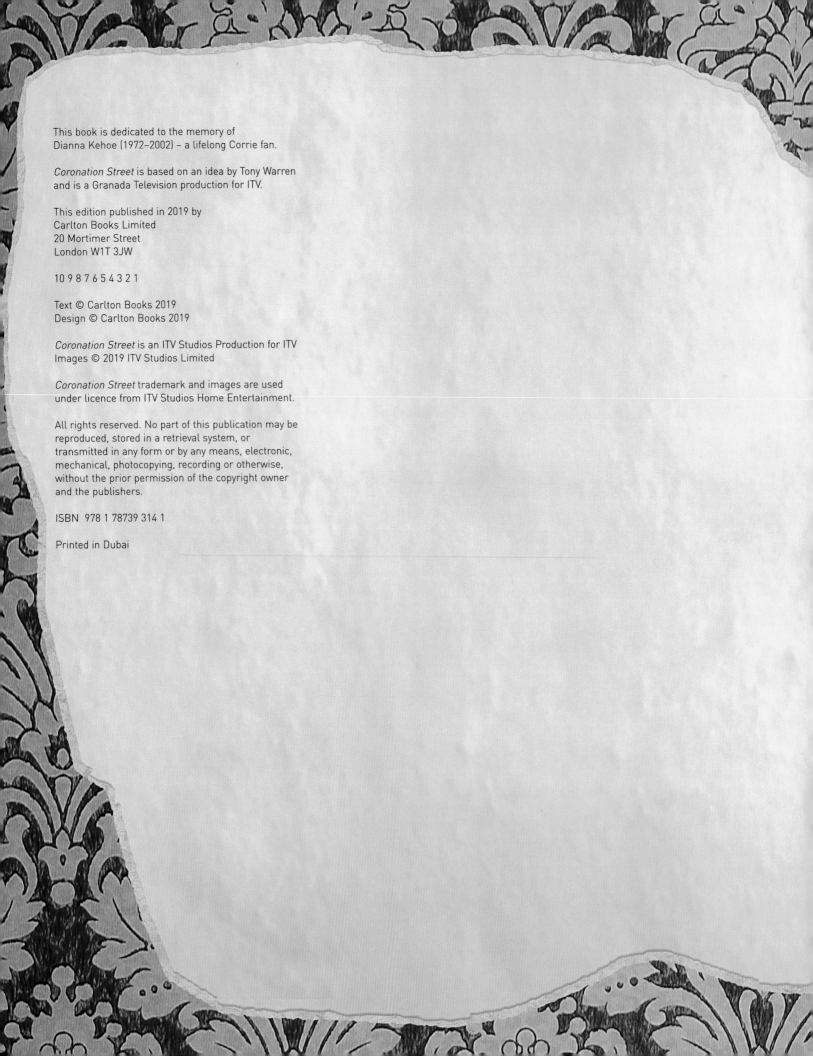

This book is dedicated to the memory of
Dianna Kehoe (1972–2002) – a lifelong Corrie fan.

Coronation Street is based on an idea by Tony Warren
and is a Granada Television production for ITV.

This edition published in 2019 by
Carlton Books Limited
20 Mortimer Street
London W1T 3JW

10 9 8 7 6 5 4 3 2 1

ISBN 978 1 78739 314 1

Printed in Dubai

THE TREASURES OF

•CORONATION ST.•™

TIM RANDALL & SIMON TIMBLICK

CARLTON
BOOKS

itv STUDIOS
Home Entertainment

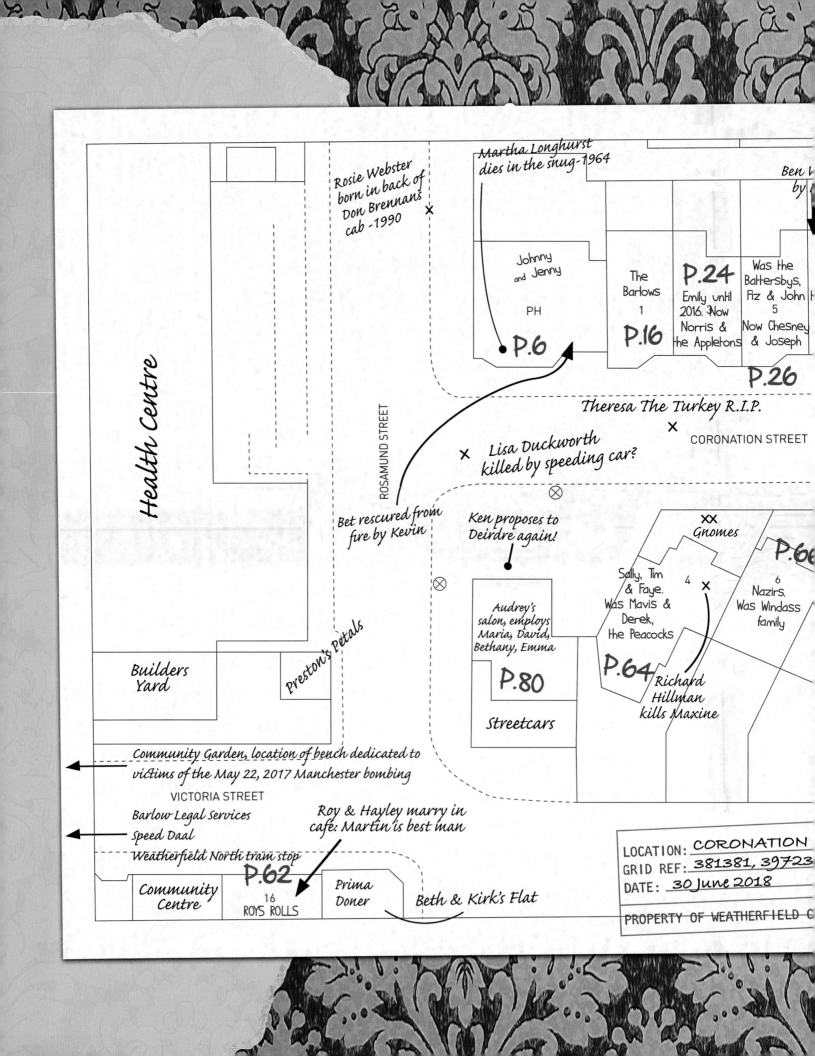

Rosie Webster born in back of Don Brennans cab -1990 ×

Martha Longhurst dies in the snug-1964

Ben ...
by ...

Johnny and Jenny

PH

P.6

The Barlows 1

P.16

P.24 Emily until 2016. Now Norris & the Appletons

Was the Battersbys, Fiz & John 5 Now Chesney & Joseph

P.26

Health Centre

ROSAMUND STREET

Theresa The Turkey R.I.P. ×

CORONATION STREET

× Lisa Duckworth killed by speeding car?

Bet rescured from fire by Kevin

Ken proposes to Deirdre again!

⊗

×× Gnomes

P.66

Sally, Tim & Faye. Was Mavis & Derek, the Peacocks

4 ×

6 Nazirs. Was Windass family

⊗

Audrey's salon, employs Maria, David, Bethany, Emma

P.80

Streetcars

P.64

Richard Hillman kills Maxine

Preston's Petals

Builders Yard

Community Garden, location of bench dedicated to victims of the May 22, 2017 Manchester bombing

←

VICTORIA STREET

Barlow Legal Services

← Speed Daal

Weatherfield North tram stop

Roy & Hayley marry in cafe: Martin is best man

P.62

Community Centre

16 ROYS ROLLS

Prima Doner

Beth & Kirk's Flat

LOCATION: CORONATION
GRID REF: 381381, 39723
DATE: 30 June 2018

PROPERTY OF WEATHERFIELD C

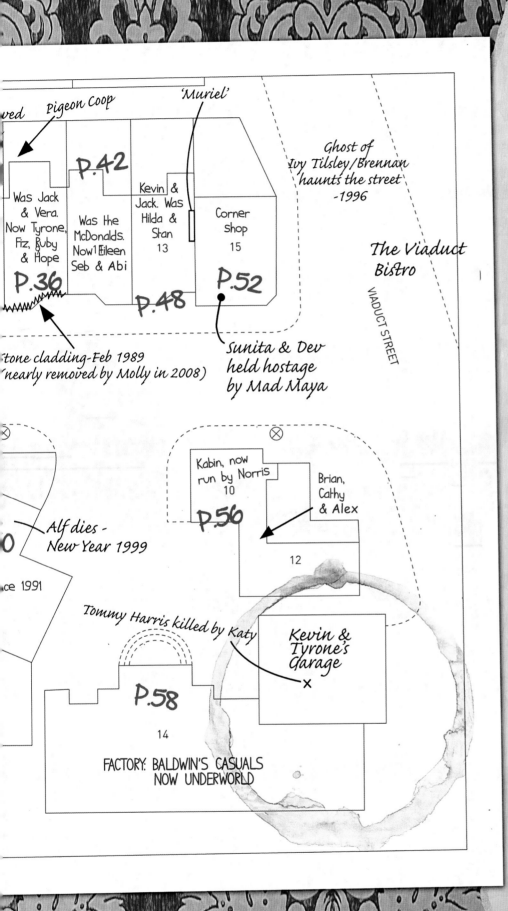

Pigeon Coop

'Muriel'

Ghost of Ivy Tilsley/Brennan haunts the street -1996

P.42

Was Jack & Vera. Now Tyrone, Fiz, Ruby & Hope

Was the McDonalds. Now Eileen Seb & Abi

Kevin & Jack. Was Hilda & Stan 13

Corner shop 15

P.36

P.48

P.52

VIADUCT STREET

The Viaduct Bistro

tone cladding-Feb 1989 (nearly removed by Molly in 2008)

Sunita & Dev held hostage by Mad Maya

Kabin, now run by Norris 10

Brian, Cathy & Alex

P.56

12

Alf dies - New Year 1999

ce 1991

Tommy Harris killed by Katy

Kevin & Tyrone's Garage

P.58

14

FACTORY: BALDWIN'S CASUALS NOW UNDERWORLD

Contents

I live in a very funny area, me. I'm quite normal compared to most of them who live round our way.

VERA DUCKWORTH

Welcome to Coronation Street, that deceptively humdrum-looking corner of Weatherfield where, for six eventful decades, the gossips have always had something to tittle-tattle about. From Elsie's Tanner's string of gentlemen callers and Gail's murderous third husband, to Molly Dobbs and Kevin Webster's extra-curricular activities and Carla Connor's ever dramatic love life, there's never a dull moment on Britain's favourite street. In this book, we have peeled back the layers of wallpaper, house by house, to remember the generations that have lived on Coronation Street, from the evidence they have left behind. We have discovered wedding invitations, divorce papers, holiday snaps, clocking-on cards, prison visiting forms and much more. You will find here lost treasures such as the hand-written confession letters of Katy Harris and Richard Hillman, a cry-for-help postcard by Sophie Webster, Elsie's mysterious poison-pen letter and one of the few remaining posters from Rita's days as a club singer – a collector's item that I've had framed for my office wall.

Recalling some of the most dramatic moments in Coronation Street's colourful history, *The Treasures of Coronation Street* sweeps down memory lane, and offers a unique chance to get to know some of the residents of Weatherfield even better.

Tim Randall

7

More than just a backstreet boozer

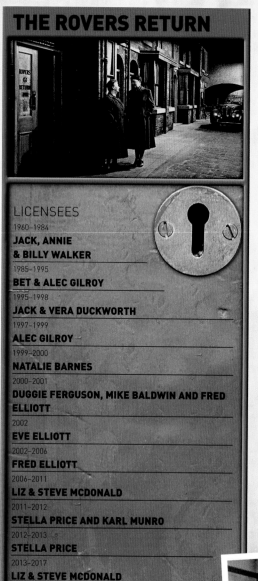

THE ROVERS RETURN

LICENSEES

1960–1984
JACK, ANNIE & BILLY WALKER

1985–1995
BET & ALEC GILROY

1995–1998
JACK & VERA DUCKWORTH

1997–1999
ALEC GILROY

1999–2000
NATALIE BARNES

2000–2001
DUGGIE FERGUSON, MIKE BALDWIN AND FRED ELLIOTT

2002
EVE ELLIOTT

2002–2006
FRED ELLIOTT

2006–2011
LIZ & STEVE MCDONALD

2011–2012
STELLA PRICE AND KARL MUNRO

2012–2013
STELLA PRICE

2013–2017
LIZ & STEVE MCDONALD

2017–2018
PETER BARLOW AND TOYAH BATTERSBY

2018–PRESENT
JOHNNY & JENNY CONNOR

Jack Walker's name might have been over the door, but there's no doubt who was boss when it came to running the Rovers Return, the pub at the heart of Coronation Street. Annie Walker would glide across the bar like royalty, seeing herself as lady of the manor, surrounded by her subjects, all of whom were just a little bit common.

One tiny sniff from Annie's disapproving nose could speak volumes. There's no disputing she was a snob, but she didn't really have much to be snobbish about – her son Billy was a waster who was always cooking up dodgy schemes, daughter Joan wasn't exactly the most loving of children and the Rovers was just a backstreet boozer. But it was Annie's empire, where she could be queen bee and reign supreme. She relished the chance to dress up as Queen Elizabeth I for the Jubilee parade or Empress Ming for the panto. And when Alf Roberts asked her to be Lady Mayoress, Annie was in her element.

Much as Annie grew to love the Rovers, she had always aspired to own a nice country pub in Cheshire. One grim day she despondently said, 'One does get rather tired of this dreary landscape. This desert of bricks and cobbled streets. Blackened chimneys piercing the sultry sky like jagged teeth.'

So Annie was forever trying to take the Weatherfield boozer upmarket. In 1966 she decided a cheeseboard was the stylish accessory every pub should have. It wasn't a great success, but what really got local backs up was Annie's new rule, years later, that she would only serve customers if they

> **Three Milk Stouts – and make sure there's no lipstick on the glasses.**
> ENA SHARPLES

BELOW, FAR LEFT: **Service with a smile. Jack and Betty in 1969** BELOW, LEFT: **Annie and Hilda chat beside the bar** BELOW, MIDDLE: **Len and Stan arm-wrestle in 1965** BELOW, RIGHT: **Minnie, Ena and Martha take their usual positions in the snug in 1961** OPPOSITE: **Season's Greetings! Annie and Jack toast Christmas at the Rovers in 1962 and 1963**

were smartly dressed. Ivy Tilsley – never a woman to get on the wrong side of – threw a fit when Annie refused to serve her oily and overalled son Brian. In protest, the residents started drinking at the Flying Horse, and with takings down £15, Annie had to relent.

Another time, Annie found an old oil painting in the cellar and discovered the frame was stuffed with money and a mask. Convinced that the Rovers must have some romantic, glamorous past, she decided the pub's name should be

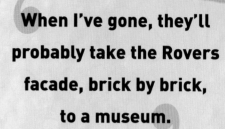

> **When I've gone, they'll probably take the Rovers facade, brick by brick, to a museum.**
>
> ANNIE WALKER

changed to 'The Masked Lady'. The brewery considered the new name, but the menfolk of Weatherfield stood up against her, and she reluctantly agreed that the Rovers would always be the Rovers.

A year later, on becoming Cutie-Beauty Cosmetics' 100,000th customer, Annie won a weekend in Paris with a French film star. After bringing back a French book for Lucille Hewitt and a beret for Jack, she went on to prepare French meals and play French records. She even considered putting tables outside the Rovers – until the regulars once again put their collective feet down, pointing out this was Weatherfield not Montmartre.

Whenever Annie got above her station, you could guarantee one of her regulars would bring her down a peg or two. She was horrified when Ena Sharples announced to the whole pub she'd kept a copy of the pre-war local rag, which detailed Annie's exploits as Lady Godiva in a pageant, when she was apparently led up Rosamund Street, naked, on a white horse. Ena assured Jack that Annie did at least wear a body stocking and wig – before the red-faced landlady stormed out of the bar.

While the locals liked a joke at Annie's expense, they also had a genuine affection for her. When she discovered the brewery was running a 'Perfect Landlady' competition, Annie drove them all mad with her uncharacteristic politeness, and they were eventually forced to admit they much preferred her when she was being high and mighty – although, much to her delight, she won. On another occasion, when the regulars threw a surprise 'This Is Your Life' party for her, Annie was in her element as the centre of attention. There were surprise appearances from her children, Billy and Joan, and a tribute from her Amateur Dramatics

ABOVE LEFT: **Elsie dreams of a life far away from Weatherfield**
LEFT: **The locals drink to birthday boy Albert's good health**

producer Mr. Nuttall, complimenting her talent and command of the stage.

But, needless to say, not all of the contributions met with uppity Annie's approval. She wasn't quite so impressed by the arrival of Mr. Stubbins, the owner of the horse she rode as Lady Godiva, who said, 'I remember we lost the procession three times. I mean, when you're leading a horse with a naked woman on it, well, you're not gonna spend much time looking where you're going, are you?'

At the end of the show, much to Minnie Caldwell and Martha Longhurst's astonishment, Ena started singing "For She's a Jolly Good Fellow", explaining herself by saying, 'Come on, it might mean another three free beers!'

When her much-loved husband, Jack, died at daughter Joan's house in Derbyshire, Annie became licensee of the pub, but, unsure of whether she could cope alone, took on a 'hostess' role and left the work to her employees. But son

Billy was never much help, and she caught him gambling with the pub's takings. So she gave grumpy Fred Gee a job as resident cellarman, and later on he doubled up as Annie's chauffeur, driving her beloved Rover 2000.

Annie also relied heavily on her other staff, including warbling cleaner Hilda Ogden, busty barmaid Bet Lynch and Betty Turpin – a strong-minded, straight-talking matronly woman, who would not always toe the party line and was once sacked by Annie, saying they were 'incompatible'. In fact, over 43 years of service at the Rovers, Betty either walked out or was sacked, then begged to return, almost as many times as she made her infamous hotpots.

Betty Turpin arrived in Coronation Street in 1969 to help out her sister Maggie Clegg, who was running the corner shop, and Betty's policeman husband, Cyril, agreed to her helping Jack out at the Rovers as well. She was never one to suffer fools, but her caring and motherly side was often seen over the years, especially in her heart-to-hearts with younger employees such as Raquel Wolstenhulme, Shelley Unwin and Bet Lynch. She liked to think of Bet as the daughter she'd never had. She was also popular with the punters, and in 1975 won Newton & Ridley's Personality of the Pub award.

Needless to say, when Annie decided to extend

ABOVE: **Mummy's boy. Billy Walker pays a visit in 1975**
BELOW: **Betty and Eddie in 1978**
LEFT: **A good old-fashioned Weatherfield singalong in 1974**

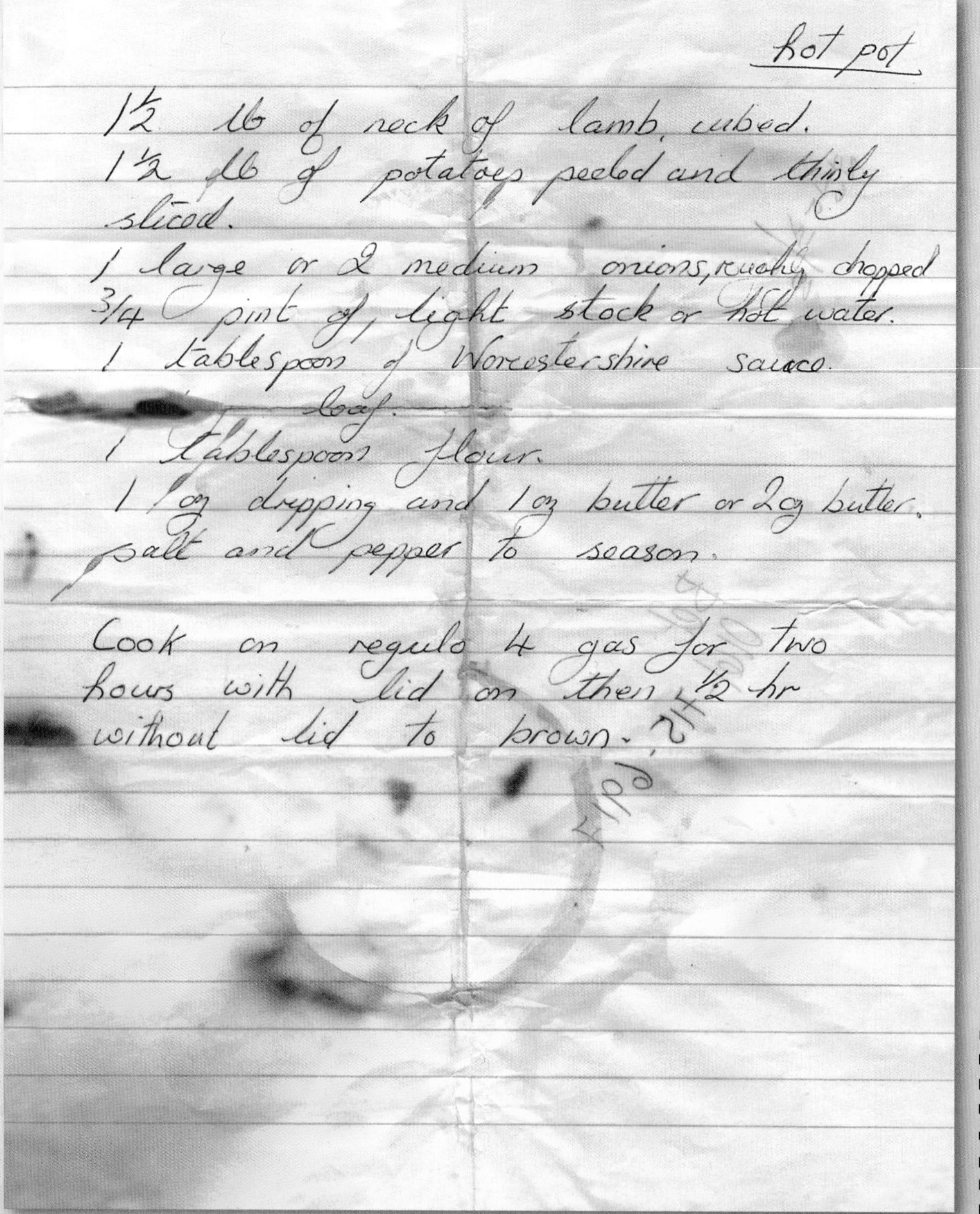

hot pot

1½ lb of neck of lamb, cubed.

1½ lb of potatoes peeled and thinly sliced.

1 large or 2 medium onions, roughly chopped

3/4 pint of light stock or hot water.

1 tablespoon of Worcestershire sauce.

~~loaf.~~

1 tablespoon flour.

1 oz dripping and 1 oz butter or 2 oz butter.

salt and pepper to season.

Cook on regulo 4 gas for two hours with lid on then ½ hr without lid to brown.

LEFT: **The secret handwritten recipe for barmaid Betty Turpin's legendary hotpot. The meaty stew remains a popular item on the Rovers menu years after Betty's passing.**

12

LEFT AND OVERLEAF: **Viva Espana! Souvenir snapshots from Bet, Rita, Deirdre, Mavis, Betty, Annie, Hilda and Emily's trip to Majorca in 1974. Bet won the holiday in a Spot The Ball competition.**

14

the food menu in 1976 and had a bell fitted so she could ring when food was ready to be served – once for Betty, twice for Bet and three times for Fred – Betty did not respond well.

But despite the larger-than-life personalities, there's always been an easy camaraderie among the staff in the pub, and when the brewery launched a new in-house magazine called *Over The Bar* it was only right that the Rovers Return should be chosen for the cover of its very first issue. Annie and Bet got all dolled up for the photographer – but while he was trying to take informal action shots, Annie insisted on royal-portrait-style posing. When the magazine was finally published, she was furious to see a much more relaxed Betty and Eddie Yeats grinning out from the cover.

Early 1977 saw a near tragedy at the Rovers

'You can't rehearse majesty, Mr. Tatlock. Either you've got it or you haven't.'

ANNIE DRESSED UP
AS QUEEN ELIZABETH I

LEFT: **A stand-off between Annie and Betty** RIGHT: **Tearful Deirdre is helped from the Rovers wreckage in 1979** BELOW: **Annie is all dressed up with nowhere to go in 1971** OPPOSITE: **The Weatherfield ladies poolside in Majorca, 1974**

16

when Deirdre Langton left Tracy outside the pub in her pram while she popped in to speak to Annie. The next thing they knew, there was a violent crashing sound – they raced outside to find a lorry had spun on its side and spilt its load of timber into the Rovers. Tracy was nowhere to be seen but was later found unharmed.

Annie was in shock, admitting to Betty she was worried that the brewery would pull the Rovers down. Thankfully they didn't, and the pub remained the focus of Annie's life until she retired – after over 40 years behind the Rovers bar – in 1984 and left Weatherfield to live with her daughter, Joan, in Derbyshire.

When Annie retired, it was only right that the management of the pub should be handed over to Bet Lynch – another strong, redoubtable woman who was never more at home than when behind the Rovers pumps. As regular Len Fairclough had put it: 'Her and those pumps go together like Morecambe and Wise.'

Bet was a brassy blonde, with a penchant for leopard skin, who had grown up in the school of hard knocks: a difficult family background; a son she gave up for adoption, who she found out 19 years later had been killed in a car crash; plus a long line of men, from Mike Baldwin to Eddie Yeats and Len Fairclough – although most of them just wanted her as a bit on the side. With all these experiences behind her, Bet was more than ready to take on the challenge of running the Rovers – no-one could have been prouder to have her name over the door.

Bet first arrived in Coronation Street in 1966, working at Elliston's PVC factory alongside Lucille Hewitt and Irma Barlow. She got special treatment, as in typical Bet style, she was sleeping with the foreman.

Four years later she reappeared in the Street,

bumping into her old friend Irma, and they decided to move into the shop flat together for £4 a week. She was then given a trial at the Rovers, and Annie soon realised Bet was an asset and let her stay – despite the fact that she was 'common'. After being mugged in 1973, she temporarily moved into the pub to recuperate.

The following year she entered the Gazette's 'Spot the Ball' competition, when Len insisted a woman could never win it. After roping in all the local girls to help, Bet scooped the prize – a holiday for two in the Bahamas. Everyone wanted to go so Annie suggested a draw, but the ladies decided against it as no-one wanted to be stuck with Hilda for a week. Eventually, the travel agent agreed to swap the holiday for a week in Majorca for eight people.

In Majorca, Annie shared a room with Emily, Rita with Mavis, Bet with Deirdre and Betty was landed with Hilda. While the other women lazed around the pool, Bet found romance with a property developer. But while she thought it was true love, he was only interested in a holiday fling. Meanwhile, Hilda overdid the sangria somewhat and was spotted on her windy hotel balcony dancing with castanets and singing "Viva España!" in an even higher voice than usual. Ten minutes later, she was back on her balcony, looking for her washing which had blown away. Bet shouted up:

'You'd better not let Stan know you've been chucking your knickers all over Palma Nova, Hilda!'

By the eighties, Bet Lynch had become as much a part of the Rovers Return as the warm ale and the hotpots themselves. So when a fire gutted the pub in June 1986, manageress Bet was, naturally, devastated. The cause was cellarman Jack's bodged attempt at changing a fuse.

Bet had been sleeping upstairs when the fire broke out. She tried to escape but was trapped by flames racing up the stairs. Overcome by smoke, she fell unconscious, and if it hadn't been for local hero Kevin Webster smashing a window and carrying her out, she would have died. The first time Bet set foot inside the gutted pub, she broke down. But, being a fighter, she soon pulled herself together and began planning the refurbishment while staying at Betty's. However, the brewery decided it wasn't worth saving the Rovers, telling a heartbroken Bet the pub was ripe for demolition. Eventually, they relented and agreed to renovate.

At the grand reopening, the pub's longest-serving staff member, Hilda Ogden, swelled with pride as she was given the honour of cutting the ribbon and declaring the new-look Rovers open. The regulars were overjoyed to be supping in their local again, but nothing could put a smile on the face of rival landlord Alec Gilroy, whose nearby

Graffiti Club had been booming during the Rovers' closure.

The following year the brewery decided they wanted to boost profits and no longer required a manageress, deciding instead to let the Rovers as a tenancy. Bet was given first refusal and tried to come up with the required £15,000, but she only had £3,000 in savings and a bank loan would have crippled her. In desperation, she turned to her old friend and sparring partner Alec Gilroy, who agreed to loan her the money.

However, profits did not improve, and unable to face the humiliation of losing the pub again, Bet disappeared. To protect his investment, Alec contacted the brewery and they allowed him to take over the licence. Two months later, he tracked Bet down to Torremolinos and proposed to her to try and persuade her to come back. To the surprise of many, in September 1987, they were married at St Mary's.

While Bet was at her best holding court behind the bar and making her punters feel at home, former theatrical agent Alec was a slimy character who'd do anything to save a few quid. As Bet put it: 'Alec, only you could think of putting up the prices on Christmas Day. You're the sort of man who'd sell tickets on a lifeboat.'

However, as a wedding present,

ABOVE, LEFT: **Bitter enemies Ken and Mike fight it out in the pub, 1990** RIGHT: **Landlady Bet reads the riot act in 1992** BELOW LEFT: **Fire destroys the Rovers in 1986** BELOW RIGHT: **Landlady Natalie teaches new barmaid Leanne to pull the perfect pint, 1999** OPPOSITE: **A lifetime of memories. The Rovers Return photo pinboard**

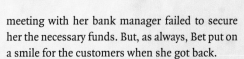

> **Well, it's a rough old pub and it needs a rough old bird to keep charge of it!**

MIKE BALDWIN OFFERS BET A COMPLIMENT

Alec generously gave Bet the Rovers tenancy back. Despite this kind gesture, the Gilroys' marriage was one of convenience rather than passion and attraction, and the odd couple wound each other up no end. Things finally came to a head in September 1992 when Alec was offered a job as Sunliners Cruises Entertainments Manager in Southampton. It was Alec's dream job – but Bet couldn't leave the Rovers and her lifelong friends, and the couple split up.

Bet stayed on, with her name back above the door, and she managed the pub until a shock announcement in October 1995. Newton & Ridley was selling six of its pubs – including the Rovers Return. The brewery wrote to confirm the sell-off and gave Bet first option to buy at £68,000. A bad meeting with her bank manager failed to secure her the necessary funds. But, as always, Bet put on a smile for the customers when she got back.

When her good mate Rita considered investing in the pub, Bet's hopes were raised. She persuaded the brewery to drop the price by £2,000, but at the last minute, Rita changed her mind and decided not to go through with the deal. Bet felt as though the ground was being pulled from under her, and the two women had a heartbreaking row. Bet accused Rita of only having money because she'd married into it, with Rita retorting that Bet had always been jealous of her because she'd married Len. The brutal rawness of their exchange ended their friendship.

Next, Bet swallowed her pride and asked Alec's wealthy granddaughter Vicky for a £66,000 loan. But she was humiliated when Vicky turned her down, before offering to buy her a small house with the promise of only charging nominal rent. Bet rounded on her, pointing out she'd loved Vicky enough to house her rent-free for four years.

Broken and angry, Bet threw Vicky out before turning on the customers and turfing them out on to the street too. She packed her bags, took one last look at the pub that had been her only real home and stepped into a taxi. After a lifetime in the same street, Bet Lynch had finally had enough of the Rovers and Weatherfield.

With Bet gone, speculation grew over who the new owner of the Rovers would be – but no-one was prepared for Jack and Vera Duckworth to step in as the next landlords, using a surprise inheritance windfall to pay for the privilege. As Betty put it at the time: 'Mrs. Walker must be turning in her grave.'

Full of her new important position in the community, Vera immediately wound Betty up by asking her to clean as well as cook. Predictably, Betty resigned in disgust. Meanwhile, Jack splashed out on a share of a dud racehorse, 'Betty's Hotshot'.

It seems it takes a string of feisty women to run the Rovers and manageress Shelley Unwin was no exception. But it was her disastrous love life that proved to be Shelley's downfall. First of all, she married Peter Barlow, only to find out he was a bigamist. But that was nothing compared to the indignities she suffered at the hands of her next beau – the controlling and leering psychopath that was Charlie Stubbs. He brainwashed Shelley against her mother and her best friend Sunita Alahan, destroyed her self-confidence and turned the once strong-minded barmaid into a gibbering wreck who developed agoraphobia and was too scared to leave her bedroom. Meanwhile,

HAPPY 90th BIRTHDAY

BETTY

LEFT AND OPPOSITE: **Betty, the Rovers Return's longest-serving barmaid, is crowned the oldest barmaid in Manchester on her 90th birthday – until 91-year-old rival Enid Crump challenges her for the title!**

Have a great day with loads of booze and cake and stuff. You're never too old to rock!
Love Becky xx

* \ | \ * | | | * | | / *
* \ | * \ | | / * | | / *
YOU'RE THE BEST BARMAID IN THE WHOLE OF
* WEATHERFIELD AND WE ALL LOVE YOU!! *
| | | * - HUGS + KISSES, | | |
* SEAN xxx

HAPPY BIRTHDAY!

Happy 90th, Betty. Keep
the hot pots coming.
– Steve

Here's to many more
happy birthdays, Betty.

Love
Michelle
x

(You'll find out
in 20 years,
Mum!)

I hope I look as good
as you when I reach 90. ←
Lots of love, Liz xx

LEFT: **A furious Vera lunges for double-crossing duo Alec and Jack in 1997**

BELOW, LEFT: **The regulars cheer in 2002**

BELOW RIGHT: **Twisted Charlie continues to destroy Shelley's confidence in 2005**

domineering Charlie was quite happily cheating on her. Thankfully Shelley got wise to what was going on and took her revenge on their wedding day when she dumped the dodgy builder at the altar, much to the delight of her mother, Bev. Shelley later found out she was pregnant with Charlie's child and, despite Bev's protestations, decided to keep the baby and moved to a Derbyshire public house where she is now landlady.

In 2006, Steve McDonald bought the Rovers from Fred Elliott – who was planning to retire to the countryside – which meant the dream had finally come true for his mum Liz, who had tried and failed to buy the pub some 11 years before.

However, life as landlady wasn't all plain sailing for Liz, partly thanks to Steve's ever complicated love life. Girlfriend and barmaid Michelle Connor's family dramas were draining, especially when she discovered that Ryan was not her biological son, having been swapped at birth. Although Liz had initially disapproved of Michelle – in the same way that she disapproved of all of Steve's girlfriends – she was furious when Steve dumped her for Becky Granger. Becky had a temper that was even shorter than Liz's skirts – and she did little to raise Liz's low opinion of her by getting so drunk that she was thrown out of her own wedding. Becky and Steve did tie the knot later in 2009, but their relationship continued to be a rollercoaster ride.

Liz herself endured a brief marriage to musician Vernon Tomlin plus various other flings. Meanwhile, there remained the jealous spectre of ex-husband Jim, hoping to demonstrate his love for Liz in the only way he knows – by beating up her boyfriends.

But, like the Rovers grand dames who had gone before her, Liz knew better than anyone that no matter what personal drama is unfolding in the back parlour, there will always be punters to serve, hotpot to dish up and a painted-on smile required front of house.

The McDonalds' reign at the Rovers came to an unexpected end in 2011 soon after the reappearance of Jim. Despite their turbulent past, Jim planned to win Liz back – and what better way to woo the lady than by buying Liz her beloved backstreet boozer!

Unfortunately, strapped for cash and unable to buy out his son Steve, dodgy Jim armed himself with a shotgun and attempted to rob a building society. His plan went horribly wrong and Jim was sentenced to seven years in prison, while disillusioned Liz decided to take a break from Weatherfield and went to live with her other son Andy in Spain.

When Steve decided to focus on his taxi cab firm Street Cars, the Rovers was under new management, with landlady Stella Price, her sulky daughter Eva and Stella's fella Karl Munro moving in. But Steve discovered there's just as much drama on the other side of the bar as there is being a regular punter...

Steve married Tracy Barlow in 2012, and the couple had their wedding reception at the Rovers. But the trouble is, anyone can wander into that pub, including a vengeful ex-wife! Armed with Tracy's medical records, Steve's third wife Becky revealed that the new Mrs McDonald had lied when she claimed Becky pushed her down the stairs at Becky's Victoria Street flat causing her to have a miscarriage. Job done, Becky went on her merry way.

During her surprise 30th birthday at the Rovers, Leanne Battersby was stunned to discover Stella was in fact her long-lost birth mum after a fling with Leanne's dad Les years earlier.

But while Stella was busy making up for lost time with Leanne, Karl's eye began to wander, and he began an affair with barmaid Sunita Alahan. When the love-cheats were eventually exposed, Stella kicked out Karl and demanded he sign over his half of the pub.

> Steve: **You're a bit of a loose cannon.**
> Becky: **With plenty of balls, so back off!**

However, still in love with Stella, twisted Karl attempted to frame her new builder boyfriend Jason Grimshaw by starting a fire in the pub cellar. But he was caught in the act by Sunita and during a furious struggle, Sunita was knocked unconscious and left to die in the blaze.

Karl was hailed a hero when he saved Stella from the burning building, and the pair eventually got back together and married. But on their wedding day, guilty Karl confessed to his crimes and asked Stella to go on the run with him. While he was holding her hostage at the pub, Stella convinced Karl to give himself up, and he was arrested for arson and murder.

In 2015, with the McDonalds now back at the helm, the Rovers was at the centre of a shock takeover bid by Steve's now ex-wife, Tracy. With no love lost between her and ex-mum-in-law Liz, Tracy started an affair with Liz's new man, Tony Stewart, and together they successfully plotted to con cash-strapped Steve and his fifth wife Michelle Connor out of their half-share of the pub, purchasing it under the guise of a bogus company called Travis Ltd. Intending to swindle Liz out of the remaining 50% of the business, Tony talked her into selling up and moving to Spain with him. However, Tracy's dream of becoming Queen of the Rovers was shattered when Liz found out about the affair and called off the sale, eventually tricking Tony into giving back Steve's share too.

Alarm bells rang when recovering alcoholic Peter Barlow announced he wanted to buy the Rovers from Steve and Liz in 2017. Would he be able to avoid temptation, having fallen off the wagon so many times before? Surprisingly, Peter steered clear of the demon drink, happily devoting himself to family life with his son Simon and fiancée Toyah Battersby. However, Toyah's desperation for a baby of her own led her to embark on a hare-brained scheme whereby Eva Price gave birth in secret, with Toyah passing off the newborn baby as the one she and Peter were expecting via a surrogate. Peter was besotted by baby Susie, so when Toyah admitted her deception, it proved the death knell for their relationship, and Peter moved out, insisting they sold the Rovers and went their separate ways.

In summer 2018, Johnny Connor and his wife Jenny, herself a former Rovers barmaid, became the latest owners. Under their watch misbehaving locals have been barred, there have been slanging matches, thrown drinks, ill-advised love affairs and medical emergencies, so it's reassuring to know that the Rovers' long-standing traditions continue to be upheld.

ABOVE, LEFT: **Charlie's reign of humiliation continues with his slimming chart for Shelley**
BELOW: **Reformed boozer Peter and Toyah begin running the Rovers in 2017**
BELOW RIGHT: **Tracy becomes Steve's 4th wife in 2012 – but the marriage was short-lived!**
BELOW LEFT: **On her 30th birthday in 2011 Leanne discovers Stella is her biological mum**

23

Osgood & Bertrams

Estate Agents & Surveyor   Trading since 1973

Weatherfield office:12 High Street,Weatherfield,Gtr Manchester GM1 5SC.Tel: 0161 715 1901

The Rovers Return
Weatherfield
GM1 5SC

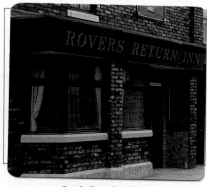

£68,000

Osgood & Bertrams are pleased to offer to the market place a rare opportunity to buy a popular Newton & Ridley public house,complete with fixtures ,fittings and original features.
Early internal viewing is recommended to avoid disappointment.

Property comprises of:

<u>Ground Floor</u>

PUB   48ft x 37ft   with full working bar.Glass washing machine,fridge.Feature fireplace and bonquets.Jukebox.There are also customer toilet facilities.

HALL   14ft x 8ft 6in   with access to upper floor and rear yard

KITCHEN   16ft 3in x 12ft 9 in   fitted with traditional wall and base units and appliances.Door access to side of building.

LEFT AND OPPOSITE:
A bargain boozer? Weatherfield's most famous pub is put up for sale by brewery bosses at Newton and Ridley in 1995. Bet turns to Rita for help in raising the money to meet the asking price. But it's the end of both Bet's reign at the Rovers and her friendship with Rita...

LOUNGE   12ft x 10ft 3in   Feature fireplace .Access to kitchen.

Upper Floor

BEDROOM 1   11ft 6in x 8ft 9in   with loft access.single panelled radiator.Original fireplace

BEDROOM 2   12ft 2 in x 10ft 9in single panelled radiator.Small cupboard with access to boiler.
picture rail

BEDROOM 3   8ft x 7ft 4in   single panelled radiator .

BATHROOM   7ft 10in x 6ft 9in   3 piece suite in avocado.Bath with shower attachment.

There is also access through the pub to a storage cellar   12ft x 10ft 8in.

Externally
Yard with outside toilet facility and access to rear passageway

Location
From our Office proceed in a northerly direction onto High Street past the Gazette office,take a left onto
Viaduct Street,at the corner shop turn left onto Coronation Street.The Rovers Return is situated at the
end of the street on the left hand side.

If you would like to view this property please contact John Osgood on 0161 715 1901.

If you would like proffessional advice about a survey or valuation ,please contact Nigel Bertrams on
0161 715 1901.

Rd.198/RR 901

BELOW: **Ken turns food critic for the local newspaper and risks the wrath of the Rovers' Bet and Betty with this scathing review of the "below the standard" pub grub!**

Food For Thought
Our weekly dining-out Review

THE ROVERS RETURN, CORONATION STREET, WEATHERFIELD
By Ken Barlow

First impressions on entering the Rovers are favorable. The atmosphere is traditional and friendly. Mrs. Elizabeth Turpin and Miss Bet Lynch who supervise the bar give sparkling service which together with the excellent ales goes some way to compensate for the quality of the food, which alas is well below the standard expected of pub grub in these days of the bistro explosion……

Dear Deirdre

I can't begin to tell you how difficult it has been for me to make a decision in which I must hurt the people around me, particularly the woman I know has been by my side and tolerated me in more ways than I dare remember. Forgive me, but this letter is my goodbye to you, to us, to the me I can't bear to be anymore.

Deirdre, for some time now I have felt restless, trapped, unfulfilled. You have probably detected it in my changing moods. The fact of the matter is I am not getting any younger and I dread the thought that what I have now is all that my life has to offer. This is no reflection on you - not in any way at all - but these four walls at 1 Coronation Street have become like a prison to me: I yearn for something more, something different, before it is all too late! There has to be more to life than watching TV and going to the Rovers.

The truth is, I have met someone else. It was a chance meeting - certainly not prearranged - but she is an actress and she excites me, she makes me come alive. We talk about art, films, literature, all the subjects so dear to my heart, subjects which - and this was probably my fault as much as yours - I never felt able to discuss with you. I have developed feelings for her and she feels the same way about me. So it is with a heavy heart that I am saying goodbye.

You have been a wonderful wife and we have

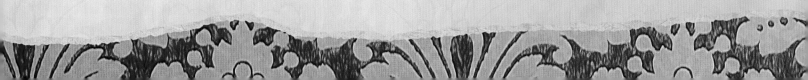

LEFT AND OPPOSITE: **Ken's confession! In 2009, Ken falls for theatre actress Martha Fraser and plans to leave wife Deirdre and sail off into the sunset aboard Martha's boat.**

been through so much together, but this is something
I must do. I sincerely hope that when you have
recovered from the shock you will meet someone else
- someone more deserving of you than I am.

Yours affectionately,

Ken
x

Born and bred in Weatherfield

Ken Barlow wasn't meant to be the man who lived in the same street throughout his life. As the first member of the Barlow clan to go to university, he was supposed to be going places. Ken was ambitious – some might even say pretentious – and determined to use his degree in history and English to get away from the Street and his working-class roots. His father Frank was a postman, and his devoted mother Ida worked in the kitchens of a large hotel.

While his football-loving brother David was his dad's favourite, politically-minded Ken yearned for his father's approval – but not at the cost of his principles. He took part in a student 'Ban the Bomb' demonstration against the Vietnam War. Frank threatened to throw him out if he went on the march, but stubborn Ken took no notice.

Ken's first chance to escape Weatherfield came when he got on the shortlist for a teaching post at a Surrey public school. But as he prepared to swap the back-to-backs for the rolling countryside of southern England, he fell for Valerie Tatlock. Then Ida was knocked over by a bus and killed. Days after the funeral, Ken got the Surrey job, but he turned it down, deciding to stay and look after his dad instead. To protect his father's pride, Ken lied, saying that he had failed to get the post, only for Frank to express disappointment in his son.

Instead, Ken took a local job at Bessie Street Primary and sold his scooter to pay for the wedding to Val. They married at St Mary's Parish Church, honeymooned in London and then moved into No 9 – which they bought from the Cheveskis for £560. In 1965, twins Peter and Susan were born and, six years later, it looked like Ken was finally going to leave Weatherfield for good when he was offered a job as Head of the Liberal Arts Department at a private school in Montego Bay, Jamaica. The Barlows agreed this was too good an

№ 1 CORONATION ST.

RESIDENTS

1960–1984
ALBERT TATLOCK

1972–PRESENT
KEN BARLOW

1981–2014
DEIRDRE BARLOW

1981–2018
TRACY BARLOW

1995–1996
DENISE & DANIEL OSBOURNE

2000–2009
BLANCHE HUNT

2004–2018
AMY BARLOW

2014
ROB DONOVAN

2015–2016
ROBERT PRESTON

2018–PRESENT
PETER & SIMON BARLOW

ABOVE, TOP: **Ken and Uncle Albert have a heart-to-heart in 1972** ABOVE: **Proud parents Val and Ken show off the twins in 1965**
RIGHT: **Ken and dad Frank tuck into breakfast, 1961**

> **6** Ken doesn't want to stare at thongs all day – the man's an intellectual. **9**
>
> BLANCHE WHEN HOUSE GUEST
> LIZ McDONALD HANGS OUT HER SMALLS

> Me and Ken, it's like we were always meant to walk beside one another.
>
> **DEIRDRE**

opportunity to miss. It was their new start.

But tragedy struck. On their last night in Weatherfield, as Val got ready for their farewell party, she was electrocuted by a faulty hair dryer. The house was gutted, and Val died in the blaze.

After the untimely death of his mother, this was the second of many tragedies to befall Ken, for whom life has never been straightforward. He's had more jobs than most people have had hot dinners – from teacher, newspaper editor and warehouse manager to agony aunt, ('Dear Hermione', in the *Weatherfield Gazette*), taxi driver and trolley pusher at Freshco.

Perhaps Ken's most unlikely profession was as a male escort for the Golden Years Escort Agency, run by Alec Gilroy. It seemed smoothie Ken had found his niche until one of his clients, Babs Fanshawe, died halfway through their meal.

Despite his constant flings and marriage-wrecking affairs, there has been only one true love of Ken's life – Deirdre. They were on and off more times than Blanche's spectacles, but as the years went by, the perfect pair realised they belonged together, and they finally found their happy ending when they tied the knot for the second time in April 2005.

Deirdre Hunt arrived in Coronation Street in the early seventies as a secretary in Len Fairclough's builder's yard. Always one to follow her heart in the hope of a better life, Deirdre was never short of male interest. She pulled out of marriage to Billy Walker only days before their wedding (much to her prospective mother-in-law Annie's relief) and, only two months later, married builder Ray Langton instead.

In March 1977, their daughter Tracy was born, but Ray and Deirdre's happiness was to end there. Deirdre was attacked one night under the viaduct, leaving her depressed and suicidal. The following year, Ray had an affair with a waitress and left Weatherfield and his wife and child for a new life in Holland. Nearly 27 years later, after discovering he was terminally ill, he arrived back in Coronation Street to be reconciled with his estranged daughter – his dying wish.

Ken and Deirdre first married in July 1981. Her boss, Alf Roberts, gave her away and the family moved into No.1 to live with Uncle Albert, who was now in poor health. Ken adopted Tracy and the future looked rosy. But, two years later, Deirdre realised marriage to Ken was hardly a barrel of laughs and yearned for some excitement. She had an affair with Mike Baldwin but after much indecision (and fisticuffs between her two beaus) she stayed with Ken until he had an affair with his secretary Wendy Crozier, and they divorced in 1992.

After that, Deirdre loved and lost her Moroccan toy-boy husband Samir (attacked whilst on his way to give Tracy a kidney), and Ken hooked up with hairdresser Denise Osbourne and had a son, Daniel.

29

RIGHT: **Ken officially adopts his wife Deirdre's daughter Tracy, whose birth dad Ray Langton had run off years earlier. If only Ken knew how much trouble he was signing-up for!**

CERTIFIED COPY OF AN ENTRY IN THE
RECORDS OF THE GENERAL REGISTER OFFICE

Application Number _002854_

(1) Date of entry	(2) Name of adopted child	(3) Sex of adopted child	(4) Name and surname, address and occupation of adopter or adopters
Nineteenth June 1986	Tracy Lynette	Female	Kenneth BARLOW (Newspaper Editor) and Dierdre BARLOW his wife both of 1, Coronation Street Weatherfield, Salford, Manchester.

CERTIFIED copy of an entry in the Adopted Children Register mantained at the General Register Office, under the seal of the said office, the **19th** day of **June** 19 **86**

WARNING: THIS CERTIFICATE IS NOT EVIDENCE OF IDENTITY

Given at the

WEATHERFIELD REGISTER OFFICE

(5)	(6)	(7)
e of birth f child	Date of adoption order and description of court by which made	Signature of Officer deputed by Registrar General to attest the entry
ty Fourth ry 1977	Eleventh June 1986, Weatherfield County Court	Mary R. Hadfield

ne WEATHERFIELD REGISTER OFFICE,

> **She could fill a Sunday paper on her own. There's a lot goes on behind them glasses you don't know about.**
>
> VERA DUCKWORTH ON DEIRDRE

OPPOSITE: **A full house in 1982**

ABOVE: **Deirdre and first husband Ray Langton with baby Tracy in 1977**

BELOW, LEFT: **Another of Ken's affairs – secretary Wendy Crozier in 1989**

BELOW RIGHT: **Doorstep drama – Ken discovers Mike and Deirdre's fling, 1983**

But when it comes to picking the wrong love interests, it has to be Deirdre who wins the top prize. On a girls' night out in 1997, she bumped into dashing stranger, Jon Lindsay. On paper he was the perfect catch – a good-looking, wealthy pilot. Who could blame Deirdre for falling for him? Unfortunately, it soon transpired that Jon's only experience with aeroplanes was watching them take off from the airport tie shop where he actually worked.

Eventually, he came clean to Deirdre, saying he'd just wanted to impress her, so she forgave him and the pair went ahead with their wedding plans. They moved into a detached house in the leafy suburbs of Manchester, and Deirdre handed him her £5000 life savings. While happily living in ignorant bliss, what Deirdre didn't know was that Jon was a con artist who had stolen another man's identity so he could obtain credit cards to fund their glamorous lifestyle. He'd also failed to mention to smitten Deirdre that he already had a wife and children.

When she found out about Jon's other family, distraught Deirdre tried to get her money back from their joint account, but her card was refused and she soon found herself arrested for deception and fraud. Unable to prove she wasn't in on the scam, or convince the police of Jon's dodgy double life, Deirdre was arrested and sentenced to 18 months in jail. Her wrongful imprisonment sparked a national campaign to 'Free the Weatherfield One', headed up by ex-husband Ken, friends Liz and Emily, and ex-boyfriend Mike, who paid £10,000 towards Deirdre's defence.

After three weeks in the slammer, sharing a cell with gobby Jackie Dobbs – Tyrone's mum,

33

RIGHT: **Ken, Liz, Emily and Mike launch the national campaign, "Free The Weatherfield One!" after Deirdre is framed by conman Jon Lindsay and sent to prison for fraud in 1998.**

Hermione Fairfax

YOUR LETTERS

TODAY... THE MAN WHO CANNOT FORGIVE

DEAR HERMIONE

I am very fond of a man I have been going out with for some time. Recently we split up because he is an undertaker and I discussed some of his work with friends of mine and he said I betrayed his confidence. I have tried apologising but he won't listen. I am a mature lady living with my daughter and her boyfriend.

DEAR UNKNOWN

"The man who cannot forgive is best forgotten."

This man is history, so if it's love you're looking for then seek out pastures new. if you move into sheltered housing you would be able to mix with many more people of your own age.

LOVE RAT WHO WRECKED OUR FAMILY...

DEAR HERMIONE

Recently my best friend caught me necking with her boyfriend of 3 years. He knows he is good looking and I have fancied him from the first time saw him. When he came on to me at a party we were all invited to, I couldn't resist - I was all over him like a rash. But I now realise my friendship is more important. What can I do to make my best friend see this.

DEAR MISS KISS

If you put your feelings in writing to your friend, this will give her a chance to let what you say sink in - it has worked for me in the past. If you put your feelings in writing to your friend, this will give her a chance to let what you say sink in - it has worked for me in the past.I you put your feelings i

35

who was inside for GBH – and protesting her innocence, Deirdre was released when another of Jon's duped women came forward and gave evidence against him. Meanwhile, Jon was taken into custody.

If anything, Deirdre's prison ordeal brought her and Ken closer together. After some matchmaking by her mother Blanche during a visit in 1999, the pair realised they still had feelings for each other and a year after she was released from jail – just before Ken's 60th birthday – Deirdre Rachid moved back into No.1.

That same year, Blanche was back full-time, much to Ken's annoyance, and the tiny terrace became even more crowded in 2002, when Christmas dinner was interrupted by the surprise return of troublesome Tracy from London. She'd left husband Robert, claiming he'd had an affair, but it turned out she was the one who had been unfaithful.

Within hours of being back on the Street, Tracy bedded shopkeeper Dev Alahan, the man her mum had drunkenly slept with a year before. When Tracy found out about Deirdre's infidelity, she spitefully let the cat out of the bag to Ken – who threw her out of the house, while Deirdre begged his forgiveness once again.

In June 2003, Tracy had a one-night stand with Steve McDonald while he was separated from wife Karen – probably the biggest mistake of Steve's life. Around the same time, Tracy drunkenly bet Bev Unwin she could bed Roy Cropper. Typically,

where Tracy is involved, what started out as a bit of fun turned into something much more cruel and manipulative. While Hayley was out of town, Tracy drugged Roy at Shelley and Peter's wedding and pretended they had slept together.

A couple of weeks later, Tracy discovered she was pregnant and insisted Roy was the father. She agreed to sell Roy and Hayley the baby – whom they called Patience – for £25,000 and happily robbed them of their life savings. Just as Roy began to bond with his daughter, Tracy stormed into Karen and Steve's church wedding and finally told the world that Steve was the real father. Taking the baby back from the Croppers and renaming her daughter Amy, she then set about doing everything she could to destroy Karen and Steve's marriage – and she succeeded, using Amy to drive a wedge between them.

Ken and Deirdre must have wondered whether their own chequered romantic history had anything to do with their daughter's rather ruthless attitude to relationships.

ABOVE: **The residents of No.1 in 2004** LEFT: **Picnic in the park for Ken and teenage Tracy** BELOW, LEFT: **Deirdre with double-crossing 'pilot' Jon Lindsay** BELOW: **Taking the stand – Deirdre protests her innocence in 1998**

36

> **Good looks are a curse, Deirdre. You and Kenneth should count yourselves lucky.**
>
> BLANCHE

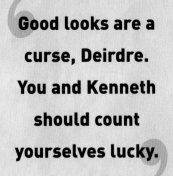

WEATHERFIELD COUNCIL

NAME _Blanche Hunt_

ADDRESS _1 Coronation Street_
Weatherfield GM1 5SC

Pass to enable old age pensioner with
FREE travel
on all Weatherfield transport

D.O.B. _27.3.1926_

Signature _B. Hunt_

BUS PASS

BELOW: **The McDonald-Barlows on the box in 2004** BELOW LEFT: **The bookies on fire in 2009**

When Tracy was arrested and then found guilty of the murder of cheating boyfriend Charlie Stubbs in 2007, their daughter's shocking behaviour looked set to destroy Ken and Deirdre's relationship yet again, with a broken-hearted Deidre desperate for someone to blame for what had happened and deciding that put-upon Ken was the man for the job. Soon Deirdre's constant sniping became too much for Ken and after an emotional farewell to mother-in-law Blanche, he moved out of No.1 and into a B&B. Feeling a failure as a father, Ken re-established contact with Denise Osbourne, who had sent him a card after reading about Tracy's imprisonment, in order to try and make a better job of fatherhood with his long-lost son, Daniel.

Understandably, when Deirdre found out Ken was now sleeping on Denise's sofa, it looked like the Barlows' marriage was over for good. However, as Denise made a clumsy pass at Ken over a bottle of wine, he pulled away, realising that Deirdre was still the only woman for him.

Ken's loyalty was tested once more when he met attractive actress Martha Fraser, who invited him on board her barge – where they enjoyed stimulating conversation over expensive bottles of wine. Martha's love of the arts offered Ken an exciting escape from the daily drudgery of life with Deirdre and this time he got as far as penning a farewell letter to his wife. But at the last moment, he backed out again, leaving Martha to sail off into the sunset.

In truth, Ken soon had more than enough on his plate at home. Peter the bigamist had returned to Weatherfield with young son Simon and bought the betting shop. But Peter was drinking heavily and after one boozy session caused a fire at his flat, which nearly killed Simon, Ken encouraged him to get help for his alcoholism. When Peter found the love of a good woman – reformed prostitute and arsonist Leanne Battersby – he vowed that his drinking days were behind him. Then Simon's other granddad, George, turned up, offering to finance Peter and Leanne's dream of

FRIDAY 12

Top of the Tree ITV1 7.30pm
'What does money do?' Altogether now: 'Grow on trees, Dave!' The McDonald-Barlow family play for a luxury car in the fast paced general knowledge quiz show.

DEIRDRE'S HEN NIGHT 2005

opening a bar. Ken feared the venture would be a disaster, and he was right. Before the bar even opened for business, Peter fell off the wagon with a resounding thud, leaving Ken and Deirdre to pick up the pieces.

Although Ken is forever complaining about his dull existence – duller still following the death of his old sparring partner Blanche in 2010 – there must be times when even he wishes life were a little quieter at No.1.

Tracy's release from prison in 2010 brought a whole lot of trouble to Ken and Deirdre's doorstep. She began a rivalry with Steve's new wife, Becky, which eventually saw Becky go on the rampage at No.1 with a sledgehammer – convinced Tracy had reported her to Social Services, causing her to lose custody of her nephew, Max.

But while one member of the Barlow family was

out of prison, another was headed for the slammer when Peter was found guilty of murdering his barmaid lover, Tina McIntyre. Meanwhile, Tracy was unknowingly engaged to Tina's real killer, Rob Donovan, who absconded from the police on their wedding day.

After yet more arguing during a family dinner, Deirdre furiously threw a trifle at the living room wall and then fled to the Peak District to stay with her friend, Bev Unwin. But Ken and Deirdre's separation sadly turned out to be permanent when Deirdre died just as she was to return home, where her family and friends were planning a surprise 60th birthday party for her.

The Barlow family was broken by Deirdre's death, and for a while Ken and Tracy were at odds after he discovered Deirdre stayed away from Weatherfield because she couldn't cope with her troublesome daughter. But hope arrived in the shape of Tracy's first husband Robert Preston, now a restaurant chef. Ken approved when Tracy and Robert got back together and even compared their relationship to his and Deirdre's.

A medical emergency reunited the bickering Barlows when Ken collapsed from a stroke in late 2016. Tracy, her daughter Amy, Peter, his son Simon, Ken's grandson Adam Barlow and his estranged son Daniel Osbourne all visited Ken in hospital, and for a while it was a full house at No.1 as everyone put aside their differences to help with Ken's recovery.

Unfortunately, nobody has perfected the recipe for long-lasting family harmony. Having survived his stroke, Ken was pushed down the stairs by an unknown assailant in 2017, having made enemies of his entire family, apart from Eccles the dog. Daniel eventually confessed to the crime. But to the complete shock of everyone, Ken lied to the police to clear Daniel's name, partly took the blame for what happened, and has since repaired his relationship with Daniel through their shared love of literature and classical music.

That said, Ken is often reminded, just because extended family members move out of No.1 it doesn't mean they won't come knocking on the door again. So it's always wise to have clean bed linen ready for any unexpected, and often unwanted, overnight guests!

OPPOSITE ABOVE: **Second time lucky? The older and wiser Barlows wed again in 2005** OPPOSITE MIDDLE: **Who was responsible for Ken's fall down the stairs?** OPPOSITE BOTTOM: **Ken with Martha Fraser** ABOVE LEFT: **Ken and Liz carry Deirdre's coffin into the church** ABOVE RIGHT: **There's silence on the Street as Deirdre's funeral hearse pulls-up outside No.1 in 2015** BELOW: **There's a full table for dinner at the Barlow house in 2016 with the return of Daniel, Adam and Peter**

BRIGHT SUMMERVILLE
48 Stanley Street, Weatherfield M10 2YT

LAST WILL AND TESTAMENT
OF BLANCHE HUNT

I, Mrs Blanche Hunt, of 1 Coronation Street, Weatherfield, England, HEREBY REVOKE all former wills and testamentary dispositions made by me AND DECLARE this to be my last will.

I APPOINT my daughter, Deirdre Ann Barlow, of 1 Coronation Street, Weatherfield, England, to be the Executor and Trustee of this my Will, provided that there should be at all times one (1) Executor and Trustee of this my Will so that in the event that my above-named Executor and Trustee shall have pre-deceased me or shall survive me but die before the trusts hereof shall have terminated or shall be unable or unwilling to act or to continue to act, I appoint, in the following order of priority, such one of the persons hereinafter named as shall not already be acting and as shall be able and willing to act to fill the vacancy so created, namely, my son-in-law Kenneth Barlow, of 1 Coronation Street, Weatherfield, England, and my granddaughter, Tracy Barlow, of Weatherfield. In this Will the expression "my Trustees" means (as the context requires) those of my Executors who obtained probate and the Trustees for the time being of any trust arising under this Will.

To my great-grandson, Simon Barlow, I bequeath my late husband Donald's antique fob watch.

To my great-granddaughter, Amy Barlow, I leave my genuine, imitation silver, music box. It should play "The Blue Danube", but I think the spring might have gone.

To my son-in-law, Kenneth Barlow, I leave my hardback Maeve Binchy novels (a proper writer). I also entrust him with the care of my faithful companion, Eccles, to feed and walk her regularly while avoiding canals, theatres, or any other places where women of ill repute may gather.

To my loyal and loving daughter, Deirdre Ann Barlow, I bequeath all of my jewellery, including brooches, necklaces and earrings. They're not worth much, but I know you've had your eye on them.

To Norris Cole, no doubt you're sitting there, hands clammy with excitement, wondering why I've asked you along, so I'll put you out of your misery. My gift to you is this: The knowledge that, for once, you've heard the news first hand and won't have to go scurrying around for it. I'd also like to take this opportunity to cancel my subscription to *Puzzler Monthly*.

And finally, the rest of my estate, including my savings of £14,000, I leave to my granddaughter, Tracy Barlow.

Deirdre

One of my earliest and most vivid memories of Deirdre, long before we got together, was when we appeared in a local production of The Importance of Being Earnest in 1974. Deirdre and I couldn't be more different, our tastes in food, politics, culture were polar opposites. Whilst I drifted away to Chopin, she washed up to the Spice Girls. Deirdre had such presence, I can't tell you how many times I walked into The Rovers without knowing she was there before hearing that distinctive laugh and seeing her presence; that throaty, joyous roar of happiness. And I'd think to myself, "well, tea will be a while yet." Deirdre wasn't a woman who wanted to set the world aflame, she was a woman who valued the life she had built for herself, and cared for those closest to her. You represent best of all what Deirdre was; she was a friend, a neighbour, a mother and a grandmother, a confidant when things were bad, and a source of love and laughter when things were good. She was a woman who spent most of her life in one street, a linchpin of the community, a role that seems to be disappearing day by day in the modern world. Deirdre could not understand the appeal of the social media, and if I got involved in some debate on Twitter, she'd look blank. "Why do you care what a load of strangers think?" she'd say, "If I want to talk about something I'll do it with my mates, in The Rovers, and I can have a drink then and all."

Her family were her priority, and she welcomed each new addition with the same enthusiasm, kindness and patience. It can't have been easy for her when we first got married and lived with Uncle Albert, and it wasn't exactly smooth sailing when her mother Blanche came to live with us; "not exactly smooth sailing", that's probably the understatement of the century. But to Deirdre, family was family, and that was that. And how she adored her two grandchildren, Simon and Amy, who've neither of them had it easy it over the years. Though with her protection and love she was able to give them what their parents often couldn't and give them the foundations in life that they needed. God bless her for that.

Why is it you never truly appreciate anything until it's taken away? Goodbye, Deirdre. I wish I'd been a better husband, and I wish I could hear that booming, life-affirming laugh, just once more.

Well, as Blanche would say, "If wishes were horses, beggars would ride".
Goodbye, my love.

LEFT: **Ken's moving eulogy dedicated to his long-time wife Deirdre who passes away in 2015. But her funeral leads to an angry showdown between Ken and his children Tracy and Peter.**

The smile of the Good Samaritan

Anyone who thought Emily Bishop was a mild-mannered do-gooder who wouldn't say boo to a goose had to think again in 1998, when the church-going widow turned eco-warrior and spent the night chained to the top of a tree in a bid to save the Red Rec from redevelopment. Gone were the beige blouses and sensible shoes, and in came camouflage combats and bovver boots. 'How do I look?' asked Emily, when she bumped into Rita in the Street. 'I wish I had a camera!' she replied, with a grin.

Rita needn't have worried, as the next day Emily's picture was splashed all over the front page of the *Weatherfield Gazette*. Always one to stand up for what she believed in, Emily and her eco-warrior nephew Geoffrey were in no doubt that as the last green space in Weatherfield, the Red Rec

deserved preservation. It turned out the site was also an area of great archaeological interest.

As the police threatened to remove Emily from the tree, saying it was no place for a woman of her age, a professor of archaeology arrived in the nick of time, brandishing a letter from the local council. The protest had been successful, and Councillor Alf Roberts's proposed 'Weatherfield Concert Bowl' was not going to be built there – much to Emily's joy.

Emily Nugent arrived in Coronation Street in 1960 and later lived at the Rovers as a paying lodger, working as an assistant at Gamma Garments. She met bright local photographer Ernest Bishop at his mother's funeral, and they married in 1972 at the Mawdsley Street Chapel. The Bishops honeymooned walking in Edale and moved into No.3 that same year.

An upstanding member of the community and a shoulder to cry on, Emily could always be relied upon to do her bit whenever it was needed – she judged the local flower show, became a leading figure in the Friends Of Weatherfield General Hospital and in 1974, with Ernest, started the popular Rovers Amateur Dramatic Association (RADA).

By 1978, Ernest was working at Baldwin's Casuals as a pay clerk, and it was there he was killed by armed gunmen during a wages raid. When Elsie Tanner broke the news to her, Emily collapsed. Her good friends Mavis Riley and

Deirdre Langton rallied round, while Ivy Tilsley started a petition to bring back hanging for murderers. But Emily refused to sign, saying she didn't believe in the death penalty.

She married again in 1980, to pet-shop owner Arnold Swain, but it was soon revealed he was a bigamist and already had a wife alive and well and living in Bournemouth. Emily felt a fool and put Ernest's ring back on her finger.

The arrival of her vegan eco-warrior nephew,

> **'I've always wanted to be stormy, passionate and tempestuous. But you can't be. Not when you're born with a tidy mind.'**
>
> **EMILY**

Nº 3 CORONATION ST.

RESIDENTS

1960–1964
FRANK, IDA, KEN & DAVID BARLOW

1968–1970
DICKIE & AUDREY FLEMING

1972–2016
EMILY BISHOP

1972–1978
ERNEST BISHOP

1979–1980
DEIRDRE & TRACY LANGTON

1983–1988
CURLY WATTS

1988–1997
PERCY SUGDEN

1997–1999
SPIDER NUGENT

2000–PRESENT
NORRIS COLE

2009
RAMSAY CLEGG

2016–2018
SEAN TULLY

2017–PRESENT
JUDE, ANGIE & GEORGE APPLETON

LEFT: **Emily and Ernest's first dance as Mr and Mrs Bishop in 1972** BELOW: **Emily with bigamist Arnold Swain in 1981** OPPOSITE, TOP: **Hard grinding author Mel Hutchwright** OPPOSITE RIGHT: **Phyllis, Curly, Emily and Percy, Christmas 1985** OPPOSITE, BOTTOM LEFT: **Norris Cole and Ramsay Clegg** OPPOSITE BOTTOM RIGHT: **Mary with her son Jude, his wife Angie and their baby son George at Roy's Rolls in 2017**

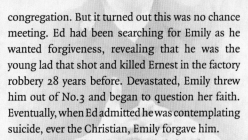

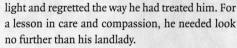

Geoffrey 'Spider' Nugent, as her lodger in 1997 gave Emily a new lease of life. She could relate to his passion for just causes and the pair became firm friends – Auntie Em even joined Spider and girlfriend Toyah Battersby in the PLO (Prawn Liberation Organisation) to save the Norwegian prawn from supermarket Firman's Freezers.

Spider may have been her flesh and blood, but he was the latest in a long line of lodgers at No.3 to have a deep affection for their self-effacing landlady. First, there was surrogate son Curly Watts, then came pensioner and former catering corps sergeant Percy Sugden. Whilst meddling

> # When you've made gravy under gunfire you can do anything.
>
> **PERCY SUGDEN**

know-it-all Percy could often rub Emily up the wrong way, he proved his loyalty by helping her through a mental breakdown in the early nineties and she appreciated his care and attention.

Her last lodger was Kabin owner and local gossip Norris Cole, and while he also had a knack of driving her round the bend, he's another lodger who looked out for Emily in times of need and was the only one who tried to stop her having any financial dealings with Richard Hillman. He was proved right after Hillman, desperate for money, tried to kill investor Emily with a crowbar. Thankfully she survived the brutal attack, but three years later there were more shocks in store for Emily when she befriended the seemingly harmless Ed Jackson, a new member of her church

congregation. But it turned out this was no chance meeting. Ed had been searching for Emily as he wanted forgiveness, revealing that he was the young lad that shot and killed Ernest in the factory robbery 28 years before. Devastated, Emily threw him out of No.3 and began to question her faith. Eventually, when Ed admitted he was contemplating suicide, ever the Christian, Emily forgave him.

Emily's kindly nature ensured that there was always a warm welcome for visitors, even if Norris – like a territorial tomcat – was less accommodating. So when Emily bumped into Jed Stone, who was recovering from a heart attack, she invited him to come and stay with her, remembering him from when he lived with Minnie Caldwell at No. 5 in the sixties.

If Norris's nose was put out by Jed's brief stay, it was twisted beyond repair by the sudden arrival from Australia of his own half-brother Ramsay Clegg, to whom he hadn't spoken in 50 years. Norris made it clear he wanted nothing to do with Ramsay, blaming him for their mother's death, and was irked when Emily took a liking to him. Ramsay made one last attempt to bury the hatchet with Norris by suggesting they move into a flat together, but when Norris bluntly refused, Ramsay booked a return flight to Australia, only to die on the journey from a brain tumour. Looking through correspondence between Ramsay and their mother, Norris finally saw him in a different

light and regretted the way he had treated him. For a lesson in care and compassion, he needed look no further than his landlady.

In 2013, when Norris rather selfishly began to worry he'd end up homeless if Emily died, Emily signed over ownership of No.3 to him but didn't charge him a penny, on the condition she could remain as a lodger. Emily enjoyed her freedom from responsibility as Norris now had the worries of paying the bills.

By 2016, it was time for Emily to take some time out for herself. After getting back in touch with her nephew Spider, Emily decided to set off on the adventure of a lifetime and join Spider in Peru, where the eco-warrior was doing voluntary work at a school. At first, Norris was against the idea, afraid such a big change would be too much for Emily. But in the end, Norris admitted Emily was the bravest person he'd ever met, and she waved goodbye to her friends and the place she'd called home for over 50 years.

Upon her return to the UK, Emily went to stay with her niece Freda in Edinburgh. Norris, who had missed her like mad, travelled north to join her but there was still a full house at No.3, with Norris having taken in Mary Taylor's long-lost son Jude Appleton, his wife Angie and their son George as lodgers.

43

Where the women rule the roost

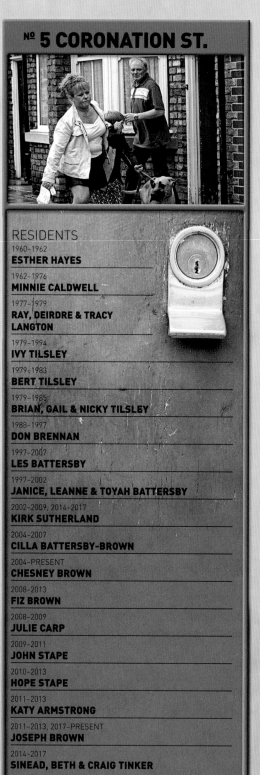

№ 5 CORONATION ST.

RESIDENTS

1960–1962
ESTHER HAYES

1962–1976
MINNIE CALDWELL

1977–1979
RAY, DEIRDRE & TRACY LANGTON

1979–1994
IVY TILSLEY

1979–1983
BERT TILSLEY

1979–1985
BRIAN, GAIL & NICKY TILSLEY

1988–1997
DON BRENNAN

1997–2007
LES BATTERSBY

1997–2002
JANICE, LEANNE & TOYAH BATTERSBY

2002–2009, 2014–2017
KIRK SUTHERLAND

2004–2007
CILLA BATTERSBY-BROWN

2004–PRESENT
CHESNEY BROWN

2008–2013
FIZ BROWN

2008–2009
JULIE CARP

2009–2011
JOHN STAPE

2010–2013
HOPE STAPE

2011–2013
KATY ARMSTRONG

2011–2013, 2017–PRESENT
JOSEPH BROWN

2014–2017
SINEAD, BETH & CRAIG TINKER

In 1997, No.5 became the noisiest house on the Street. Whether it was Les's Status Quo being played at top volume or general Battersby rowdiness, you had to pity Emily Bishop and the other neighbours.

However, back in 1962, the house was a much quieter place when Minnie Caldwell and her much-loved cat Bobby moved in. Minnie was a sweet old lady who kept a spotless house and took in the odd lodger to keep her company.

Her favourite was Scouser Jed Stone, who was forever filling her home with gear that had fallen off the back of a lorry. Minnie turned a blind eye to Jed's business affairs, and he cared about her just as much as she did him. He called her Ma and Minnie treated him like the son she never had.

Far more wary of Jed's dodgy dealings, Minnie's good friend, the formidable Ena Sharples, was disapproving of their relationship. But then Ena disapproved of everything. As Minnie said: 'I know folk think I'm simple. What I say to them is that I'd rather be simple and 'ave my pleasures than know everything and be miserable, like Ena.'

Despite being firm friends, the pair had

ABOVE: **Cheers! Minnie shares a glass or two with Emily** BELOW: **Ena, Minnie and Martha put the world to rights in 1963**

RIGHT: **Miserable Ivy keeps the faith in 1985**
RIGHT: **Brian, Ivy and Bert move in, 1979**
BELOW RIGHT: **Mourning time. Gail and Ivy**
struggle to cope with Brian's death, 1989

their fall-outs, especially when Minnie found an old letter written in 1919 which upset her greatly. It was to Ena from Minnie's late husband Armistead, declaring his love for her. But Ena explained the letter away, making it clear to Minnie there was nothing untoward involved in her friendship with Armistead.

More than anything, Minnie needed Ena to look out for her – she was far too trusting and was frequently the target of con men, who saw the kind-hearted pensioner as easy pickings. Not that she had much to pick. When she stopped taking in lodgers, Minnie's biggest worry was money. As he was in a similar position, Albert Tatlock came up with a proposition that would solve both of their problems – he asked Minnie to marry him on the basis that it would make good financial sense.

Eventually, Minnie accepted his offer. But when she discovered marrying Albert wouldn't make her better off financially, she called the whole thing off. Minnie later admitted she didn't really like Albert, or the way he drank his tea from a saucer.

In 1976, Minnie and Bobby moved, and the house became home to two of the most doom-laden clans ever to live in Coronation Street – the Tilsleys and the Brennans.

Staunch Catholic Ivy Tilsley was a woman who loved to put her two-pennyworth in – whether it was at Baldwin's Casuals where she was shop steward or disapproving of the way her beloved son Brian and his non-Catholic wife Gail lived their lives.

In 1984, after suffering a nervous breakdown,

45

> **Albert Tatlock is a luxury I really cannot afford – and besides, I don't really like him.**
>
> **MINNIE, DECLINING ALBERT TATLOCK'S PROPOSAL**

Happy Valentine's Day

To My darling Brian,

Hearts that speak can understand
What Valentine's Day is for,
For it's a sentimental time
Nobody can ignore...
So here's a special Valentine
That's sent to play its part
In wishing you great happiness
That comes from heart to heart!

With all my love
Gail x.

46

ABOVE: **Gail and her first husband Brian were together for a decade despite both of them having wandering eyes! But this card is a reminder there were some good times... in the beginning!**

RIGHT: **The infamous letter found by Minnie Caldwell in 1973, in which Minnie's husband Armistead declares he has romantic feelings for her good friend Ena Sharples.**

Ms Ena Schofield
14 Inkerman Street
Weatherfield
Lancashire

June 1919

My dearest Ena,
Forgive me for writing to you but things are such I must take up my pen. I want to thank you for your kindness and your goodness the other day. I know that lovers tiffs are thought soon passing, but, we seem strangers Minnie and myself.
Dear Ena, without your goodness my heart would be heavy to this day. Whereas I am filled with gladness. We were happy my dearest Ena and this will last. The happiness of the trees and of the grass where we walked hand in hand. This happiness will always continue. In my memory and in my heart. Such happiness is rare indeed – small wonder that I thank you. I thankyou with all my being

Indeed I am truly yours ever.

Armistead.

48

'J.D. Salinger!
Thomas Hardy!
I want *HEAT* magazine!'

HOSTAGE ROSIE WEBSTER COMPLAINS
TO KIDNAPPER JOHN STAPE

Ivy's husband Bert died whilst in a psychiatric unit. Four years later, she remarried, this time to cab driver Don Brennan. In 1989, Brian was killed outside a nightclub, and his sudden death, on top of Bert's demise, changed Ivy for good. She became an increasingly bitter woman, constantly criticising Gail about the way she was bringing up her grandson, Nicky.

Over the next few years, Ivy and Don grew further and further apart, and Ivy eventually left the Street to live in a religious retreat. In 1995, Don heard she'd died of a stroke.

She'd cut Don out of her will and left everything to grandson Nicky – on the condition he changed his surname back to Tilsley from that of Gail's second husband, Platt. The only other person to receive anything was Ivy's best mate Vera Duckworth, to whom she left £200 and a gold crucifix.

Ivy may have been dead, but as far as Vera was concerned, her spirit was very much alive and well – and living in the Street. Whilst visiting cabbie Don

at No.5, Vera popped upstairs to the loo, only to feel an eerie chill around her and then be confronted by Ivy's ghost. Trembling and speechless – surely a first for Vera – she hurried straight home to the Rovers and downed a large brandy.

With Vera convinced Ivy's ghost had followed her, Jack's interest in his new spiritual house guest increased when Betty told him a story about a busy haunted pub she'd visited. Realising he might be able to cash in on Ivy's ghostly visitations, he sold his story to a local paper, hoping it would entice more customers to the Rovers where he and Vera were licensees. Vera was unimpressed.

When she was woken one night by a strange banging in the cellar, Vera was sure it was Ivy paying a visit. But no, it was amateur ghostbuster Roy Cropper, who was determined to find out whether the Rovers really was haunted or not. 'Are you a medium?' asked Vera, with a sigh of relief. 'No, I'm a 42,' replied Roy.

Barmaid Cilla Brown – one of No.5's all-time gobbiest residents – first met divorced cab driver

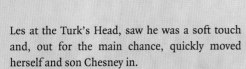

LEFT: **Fiz Brown visits John Stape in prison, September 2009**

Les at the Turk's Head, saw he was a soft touch and, out for the main chance, quickly moved herself and son Chesney in.

Happy in the Street, Chesney begged Cilla to stop seeing other men. She retaliated by threatening to put him into care if he ever breathed a word to Les. Frightened, the little boy kept quiet for as long as he could before spilling the beans. Les chucked Cilla out, but took Chesney in after his mother abandoned him.

Homeless, Cilla resurfaced weeks later, only to discover Les was back with ex-wife Janice. Determined to split them up, she played the doting mum to Chesney and faked an inheritance from a fictitious aunt. When she turned up in a stylish open-top sports car, Les couldn't resist going for a spin. Next thing he knew, Cilla was snogging the face off him in a lay-by just as Janice turned up.

Janice moved out, and smug Cilla got exactly what she wanted – a man she could twist around her little finger and a roof over her head. In 2005, the couple decided to get married, purely for the presents.

Whilst the residents took lovable Chesney to their hearts, they never felt the same way about his loud-mouthed stepdad and hard-faced slapper of a mum – especially when Cilla faked terminal cancer after finding out that Les and her best mate had slept together. She later revealed the truth before jetting off to Florida – a trip paid for by donations from local residents who believed the holiday was her last dying wish.

With Les on tour as a roadie, Cilla quit the street in 2007 when Frank Nichols (the wealthy pensioner who'd employed Cilla as his full-time carer) left her a necklace that turned out to be worth £45,000. Cilla had always been an absentee mother so, in practical terms, her vanishing act made little difference to Chesney's life: it would still be big sister Fiz who had to look after him. Reeling from boyfriend John Stape's affair with teenage temptress Rosie Webster, Fiz was understandably cautious when he tried to win her back, but slowly his persistence paid off. Even John's imprisonment for later kidnapping Rosie, couldn't dampen the flames of passion, and Fiz regularly went to see him in jail, keeping the visits a secret from the hostile Chesney. In 2009, she married John in prison, the icing on

at Underworld. A few months later, when Charlotte threatened to expose the crime, John hit her with a hammer and later turned off Charlotte's life-support machine in hospital.

Meanwhile, Fiz was all gooey-eyed over her and John's baby daughter, Hope, and failed to notice her husband's increasingly shifty behaviour. John's list of victims would extend to include Colin's mum Joy Fishwick, when she came to Weatherfield to investigate her son's disappearance. But John's killing spree came to an end when Fiz caught him digging up Colin's body at Underworld and he was forced to tell her the terrible truth.

During a confrontation on the roof of Weatherfield General Hospital, John appeared to fall to his death. However, his body was nowhere to be found, and poor Fiz found herself on trial at the Crown Court, charged with three murders.

In autumn 2011, John sneaked back to Weatherfield to help clear Fiz's namen but he was spotted and chased by Kevin Webster, and involved in a shock car crash. Rushed to

ABOVE: **Sally Webster has painted the windows of No.5 black, November 2009**

RIGHT: **A tearful goodbye for Chesney and mum, Cilla, in 2007**

the cake being the attendance of Chesney following a last-minute change of heart.

On his release, John moved in with Fiz and Chesney, but her hopes of playing happy families were dashed when Sally Webster painted the windows black in protest at John's return to the street. It was a tough start to married life but, like the previous female residents of No.5, Fiz was made of strong stuff.

Fiz found herself defending her new husband at every turn. But little did she know she'd married a murderer. When Colin Fishwick began blackmailing John for stealing his identity, John confronted him, but in the middle of the argument, Colin dropped dead. Fearing the identity fraud would send him back to prison, John and former teaching colleague Charlotte Hoyle buried the body beneath the building site

hospital, John finally confessed to the police but then suffered a fatal cardiac arrest. Fiz was released from custody and returned home.

Meanwhile, not-so-little Chesney was coming of age. He became a dad that Christmas when his teenage girlfriend, Katy Armstrong, gave birth during the local nativity play. Fiz and neighbour Anna Windass helped deliver the baby, and the young couple named their son Joseph.

Chesney loved family life, but stay-at-home mum Katy began to feel she was missing out on a wild teenage life, and after taking a mundane job serving kebabs at Prima Doner, she began an affair with her colleague Ryan Connor. Chesney discovered Katy's betrayal just after he proposed to her in front of their family and friends, and the couple swiftly broke up.

Katy decided to leave Weatherfield when her long-lost mum Linda offered her the chance of a fresh start in Portugal. Chesney let Katy take Joseph, as he knew in his heart his son would have a better life.

But tragedy struck in 2017, when Katy was killed in a car accident. Chesney travelled to Portugal and was reunited with Joseph, who he brought back home to live at No.5.

With Fiz currently settled with long-time love Tyrone Dobbs at No. 9, and Chesney having broken up with fiancée Sinead Tinker, the fast food shop manager has finally become man of the house at No.5 and is making life work as a single dad.

ABOVE LEFT: **Fiz confronts her killer hubby John on a hospital roof after he snatches their baby daughter Hope in 2011**
ABOVE: **Teenage parents Chesney and Katy dote on baby Joseph in 2012.**
BELOW: **Chesney still doesn't trust Sinead after her affair with Daniel and jilts her on their wedding day in 2018**

51

HMP Manchester Social Visits   Visits Request

Please take a copy of this form.

enter the information below

Date of Visit	6 April 2009
Morning or afternoon visit	Afternoon
Prisoner's name	John Stape
Prisoner's date of birth	16 August 1979
Prisoner's number (or state if on remand)	214
Adult Visitor's Names (aged 14 and over)	Fiona Brown
Adult Visitor's Names (aged 14 and over)	
Adult Visitor's Names (aged 14 and over)	
Adult Visitor's Names (aged 14 and over)	
Any visiting children's names and dates of birth	

Visitors Address	
House number	5
Street or road name	Coronation Street
Village or district	Weatherfield
Post town	
Post code	MM0 77G
Second Visitors Address – where different	
House number	
Street or road name	
Village or district	
Post town	
Post code	
Contact telephone number	
Any other useful information:	

52

Lost Dog!

Ring

0161 715 9674

ABOVE: **Fiona "Fiz" Brown** visits her boyfriend John after he is sentenced to two years in prison for kidnapping Rosie Webster. Fiz and John eventually get married in the prison chapel.

ABOVE: **Where is Chesney Brown's beloved pet pooch Schmeichel? The** dog was named after footballer Peter Schmeichel and remains Chesney's canine sidekick until 2011.

THE CAPRICORN CLUB
VIADUCT STREET, WEATHERFIELD

presents Weatherfield's own
RITA LITTLEWOOD

Friday 24th March 1972
Show Starts 8.30pm

LEFT: **Long before she was running The Kabin, Rita began her career as a singer during the 70s. Or as bitchy Bet puts it, "A clapped-out chorus girl!"**

Home is where the heartache is

№ 7 CORONATION ST.

RESIDENTS

1960–1964
HARRY, CONCEPTA & LUCILLE HEWITT

1982–1990
RITA FAIRCLOUGH

1982–1983
LEN FAIRCLOUGH

1986–1991
ALAN & JENNY BRADLEY

1991–2003
CURLY, RAQUEL, EMMA & BEN WATTS

1998–1999
JACKIE & TYRONE DOBBS

2004
BLANCHE HUNT, TRACY & AMY BARLOW

2004–2006
DANNY, FRANKIE, JAMIE & WARREN BALDWIN

2007–2009
MARIA & LIAM CONNOR

2009
MICHELLE & RYAN CONNOR

2009
TONY GORDON

2010–PRESENT
DEV, AADI & ASHA ALAHAN

2010–2013
SUNITA ALAHAN

2012–2013
KARL MUNRO

2015–PRESENT
MARY TAYLOR

2016–2017
ERICA HOLROYD

2017–2018
GINA SEDDON

Rita Tanner must rue the day she ever set eyes on Alan Bradley – the man who was to turn her life upside down and, ultimately, try to kill her. It's not as if Rita hadn't been through enough already. While she happily sang at Hilda and Stan Ogden's anniversary party in the Rovers, her first husband Len was killed in a motorway accident after falling asleep at the wheel of his van. To make matters worse, a grieving Rita later found out he'd been on his way back from visiting his mistress.

Despite his adulterous tendencies and long trips working away, builder Len had been the love of Rita's life, and she was unbearably lonely without him. A former foster parent, three years after Len's death, Rita decided to take in Jenny Bradley, one of her teenage paper girls who had lost her mum in a road accident. In 1986, Jenny's estranged father Alan turned up in Coronation Street to try and rebuild their relationship. He'd been out of her life for eight years and, as Alan got to know his daughter again, he became closer to Rita too.

But was it really Rita he was interested in or her Kabin of cash? When she twice refused to marry him, angry Alan sought comfort in the arms of another woman and stole the deeds to No.7. Pretending to be Len, he remortgaged the property and set himself up in a burglar alarm business with the proceeds.

As time passed, Alan's behaviour became more and more ominous. He tried to rape

6 We've all had our nightmares. We're all the walkin' wounded. It's just that some of us get more wounded than others... 9

RITA

ABOVE: **Smiles all round as Len and Rita tie the knot in 1977** BELOW: **Foster daughter Jenny Bradley causes Rita more heartache in 1986**

54

employee Dawn Prescott who, having seen regular letters addressed to Mr L. Fairclough arrive at Alan's shop, shared her suspicions about his fraudulent antics with Rita. When Rita confronted Alan, he tried to suffocate her with a pillow and only the timely return of Jenny from her 18th birthday party saved Rita's life.

Alan was jailed but, after a lengthy trial, was found not guilty and returned to Coronation Street, finding work on the building site opposite No.7. Terrorised by Alan's constant threats of revenge, Rita had a nervous breakdown and disappeared.

The police suspected Alan had murdered her and the building site was dug up as they searched for a body. Alan, meanwhile, was convinced that Rita was trying to frame him and followed Bet and Alec Gilroy to Blackpool, where they had tracked Rita down to a hotel bar. Confused and traumatised, Rita was under the illusion she was still a nightclub songstress and seemed to have blanked out recent events completely.

However, on spotting a furious Alan, something made Rita run, and he chased the terrified widow across the busy Blackpool promenade. On the other side of the road, Rita veered sharply and just missed being hit by a tram, but Alan hadn't seen it and bounced off the front. As Alan lay dead in the road, Rita's nightmarish memories of the emotional and physical abuse he'd inflicted on her came flooding back, and she collapsed into Bet's arms, sobbing hysterically.

It took Rita months to recover from her ordeal,

and she decided to put the bad memories of No.7 behind her and move into the flat over the Kabin for a fresh start.

The house's next owner, geeky Curly Watts, first set foot on Coronation Street in 1983. A bin man employed by the local council, his messy hair and thick glasses marked him out from the crowd.

A course in business studies changed Curly's life, and by the time he bought No.7 from Rita, he had gone up in the world. He was now an assistant manager at local supermarket Bettabuy, learning the trade under the tutelage of eccentric boss Reg Holdsworth – a bewildering jobsworth who lurched from one crisis to the next. As Curly once sighed to Betty in the pub: 'Madman or genius, Betty? I just don't know – and I work with him every day.'

Whilst his home life and career were settled, Curly's love life was a different kettle of fish. In fact, it was nothing short of disastrous until he met his second wife Emma, a policewoman, in 2000, and the couple moved to Newcastle with their two-year-old son Ben three years later.

Curly's first girlfriend was machinist Shirley Armitage, but they quickly drifted apart. It took him longer to get over his broken engagement to shelf-stacker Kimberley Taylor, although he was relieved to be shot of her scarily Victorian 'Mummy and Daddy'. Kimberley ended their relationship because of Curly's numerous attempts to woo her into his bed before their wedding night, something that was strictly off the agenda.

The next woman to win Curly's heart was a very different Bettabuy employee – Raquel

ABOVE LEFT: **Death by tram in Blackpool, 1989** ABOVE: **Fatal attraction. Alan Bradley keeps an eye on Rita in 1988**
BELOW: **Store Wars. Vera, Reg, Kimberley and Curly in the aisles of Bettabuy in 1989**

FRESHCO

NORMAN WATTS

> **You're great when it comes to duty rosters or displaying tins of soup – probably one of the best. You're just not for me any more.**
>
> RAQUEL FINISHES WITH CURLY

Wolstenhulme. The pair became close after Curly comforted Raquel when she failed to win the Miss Bettabuy contest at a posh Derbyshire hotel. Upstairs in Raquel's room one thing led to another, but love failed to blossom between them.

It was back to the drawing board for Curly, and more brief encounters followed – usually after several bottles of red wine – with the likes of fashion student Angie Freeman and Maureen Naylor, the soon-to-be Mrs Reg Holdsworth. Then there was Anne Malone, the ambitious colleague who had a crush on Curly. When he made it clear he wasn't interested, she manically stalked him before trying to get him sacked for sexual harassment.

But deep down, Curly was still besotted by ditzy blonde Raquel, and in 1995 they finally tied the knot. A one-time model who wore her heart on her sleeve, Raquel clearly still had feelings for her ex, Des Barnes. But after she had discovered Des two-timing her with fellow barmaid Tanya Pooley, she ran back to the safety of dependable Curly's arms. And while she wasn't in love with him, she cared about him deeply.

But after just eleven months, Raquel fled Weatherfield to work as an aromatherapist in Kuala Lumpur, leaving Curly heartbroken. Deep down however, he understood that Raquel could never love him enough to stay.

So, three years later, while the other Street residents were celebrating the arrival of the new millennium, the last person Curly expected to turn up on his doorstep at two in the morning was his estranged wife. Understandably, he was lost for words, but he sat and listened sadly as Raquel explained she wanted a divorce so she could marry her new lover, a Frenchman named Armand. And there was another shock in store when Raquel showed Curly pictures of her two-year-old daughter Alice, dropping the bombshell that Curly was the father. She'd discovered she was pregnant shortly after arriving in Kuala Lumpur but kept the news from Curly knowing he'd beg her to return. After an emotional heart-to-heart, Curly finally agreed to give Raquel her freedom.

The next residents of No.7 were the Baldwin clan headed by Dad, Danny, who had moved up to Weatherfield in 2004 from Essex to run Underworld with his 'Uncle' Mike. Then followed one of the street's most incestuous set of affairs. Danny ended up cheating on his wife, Frankie, with his son Jamie's girlfriend, Leanne Battersby. When a broken-hearted Frankie found out, she dumped

ABOVE: **Decision time for Raquel in 1995. Curly or Des?** FAR RIGHT: **Naughty Danny cheats with Leanne in 2005** MIDDLE RIGHT: **Liam with Carla** RIGHT: **Curly and second wife Emma show off baby Ben, 2001**

Danny and Jamie disowned his father. Then Frankie and her stepson Jamie began their own illicit affair which resulted in a horrified Danny – for once lost for words – trying to kill his son by drowning him in the canal. Not surprisingly, when the Baldwins were bedhopping, the locals were having a field day.

No.7 remained in Underworld hands when, following the Baldwins' departure, Liam Connor moved in with hairdresser Maria Sutherland. It should have been cosy for them, with the baby she was expecting, but there was always an elephant in the room – Liam's sister-in-law Carla. Although Maria did marry Liam, she was convinced that he really wanted to be with Carla, and that insecurity intensified when their baby son was stillborn. While a grieving Maria was trying to decide whether her marriage was worth saving, Liam wasted no time falling into Carla's welcoming arms.

Maria and Liam managed to resolve their problems, but no sooner did she fall pregnant again, he was killed on the orders of Carla's fiancé, Tony Gordon, as punishment for the affair. Maria accused Tony of murdering her husband, but her ramblings were dismissed as the actions of an unstable widow.

So vulnerable was Maria, that she started to fall for Tony, who even helped deliver Liam's baby. He moved in and announced their engagement, to the disgust of Liam's parents. Then the truth came out about Tony's involvement in Liam's death. Maria was devastated – another heartache inside No.7.

Dev Alahan bought the terrace house from Maria in 2010 when she moved into the flat above Audrey's salon. Dev had recently reunited with his ex-wife Sunita, and the couple moved in with their twin children, Aadi and Asha.

But they quickly fell out with the neighbours when they accused childminder Claire Peacock of abuse after Aadi collapsed with a head injury that caused bleeding to the brain. The twins were placed into foster care during an investigation into the boy's injury, until naughty Simon Barlow eventually confessed he pushed Aadi over during a fight and he hit his head.

Dev's daughter Amber Kalirai unexpectedly turned up on the doorstep in the summer of 2011, having been kicked out of university. But lazy Amber's presence around the house soon got on Sunita's nerves, especially after she hosted a party at No.7 while Aadi and Asha were asleep upstairs. Dev blamed Sunita for Amber's eventual departure from Weatherfield, and he unknowingly drove Sunita into the arms of Rovers landlord, Karl Munro.

Dev had wanted to marry Sunita again. But it was not to be – Sunita's ill-fated affair with Karl resulted in her death, and Karl's arrest for arson and murder.

After Sunita's death, Mary Taylor moved in as the children's nanny but also developed a close bond with their dad. Although not interested in Dev romantically, Mary's nose was still pushed firmly out of joint when he began diverting his attentions to factory machinist Julie Carp, who made a play for the local businessman and enjoyed a short-lived romance with him.

Since then, Mary has stuck around to keep an eye on the Alahan family, often approving but mostly disapproving of Dev's various lady friends who have included his shop assistant Erica Holroyd and Sally Metcalfe's younger sister, Gina Seddon.

ABOVE: **Jamie, Frankie, and Warren. The Baldwin clan arrive in the Street, 2004**
BOTTOM LEFT: **Tony Gordon confesses to Carla that he had Liam killed, 2009**
BELOW: **Dev informs the twins of Sunita's death in 2013**

57

For better or for worse – the Duckies

No 9 CORONATION ST.

RESIDENTS

IVAN & LINDA CHEVESKI
1961

KEN & VALERIE BARLOW
1962–1968

LEN FAIRCLOUGH
1968–1982

RAY LANGTON & JERRY BOOTH
1968–1975

RITA FAIRCLOUGH
1977–1982

CHALKIE WHITELY
1982–1983

JACK & VERA DUCKWORTH
1983–1995, 2000–2009

TERRY DUCKWORTH
1983–1988

GARY & JUDY MALLETT
1995–2000

TYRONE DOBBS
2000–PRESENT

MOLLY COMPTON
2006–2010

PAUL CLAYTON
2007–2008

TOMMY DUCKWORTH
1992–1993, 2011–2012

TINA MCINTYRE
2011–2012

KIRSTY SOAMES
2011–2013

RUBY DOBBS
2012–PRESENT

FIZ & HOPE STAPE
2013–PRESENT

LUKE BRITTON
2014–2016

SEAN TULLY
2017–2018

He may be older and wiser these days, but Terry Duckworth's wicked streak is as steadfast as his mum Vera's perm. He brought nothing but anxiety to his loving parents at No.9, who lived in hope that one day he would do something to make them proud instead of his usual antics – which at best involved letting them down, and at worst saw him serve a stretch inside. The misery Terry caused over the years added up to a soul-destroying list of heartaches for his mouthy mother and pigeon-loving dad.

Terry only ever darkened the Duckworths' door when he was down on his luck. Just before another stint in jail in 1992, he brought his pregnant girlfriend Lisa Horton home to meet Jack and Vera, and they were delighted when he was released from the slammer for a few hours to marry her – even if Terry was in handcuffs until the photographs were being taken after the ceremony. Just after saying 'I do', he did a runner, only to be recaptured a few days later. A distraught Lisa was convinced that Terry had used the wedding purely as a way to escape from prison, and Jack couldn't help but agree with her. Vera, on the other hand, needed far more persuading as to her son's evil nature.

But if anything was going to show her Terry's true colours, it was his lack of love for his new offspring, baby Tommy. Jack and Vera were in their element as doting grandparents, but their happiness was short-lived when Lisa was knocked down by a speeding car outside the Rovers and died in hospital. Selflessly, Vera gave up her job to look after Tommy until Terry had completed his prison sentence, but two days after his release, to Vera's horror, Terry sold Tommy to Lisa's parents, the Hortons. He claimed Vera was too old to raise

ABOVE: **Daughter-in-law Lisa and grandson Tommy, 1992**
BELOW: **All under one roof in 1984**
BOTTOM: **No son of mine. Jack finally swings for troublesome Terry, 1993**

her photos of Terry, vowing never to acknowledge him again.

But just as Jack and Vera believed Terry couldn't stoop any lower, he did. When his ex-girlfriend, Andrea Clayton, revealed Terry's teenage son Paul needed a life-or-death kidney transplant in 2000, Terry demanded £25,000 from his parents to be the donor, before legging it with the cash. With tests revealing Jack's organs were incompatible, it was up to a distraught Vera to stand in and offer one of her kidneys to save her estranged grandson's life.

Terry reappeared in November 2001 when he was charged with attempted murder. It took being accused of a crime which he, for once, hadn't committed to make Terry reform. When Terry's innocence was proved, the Duckworths were united in celebration, perhaps for the very first time.

While Terry may never have been the perfect son to Vera, the former machinist did have other things in her life that made her heart swell with pride. The first – which changed the face of the

> **The Duckworths are primitive life forms. If you're talking evolution – they are one step above fungus.**
>
> **DES BARNES**

BOTTOM: **The winner takes it all. Vera and her brand-new Vauxhall Nova in 1986**

a child but, in reality, Terry just saw Tommy as a way to make some cold, hard cash. As the Hortons arrived to take Tommy back to Blackpool with them, Vera broke down, stunned that her own flesh and blood could be so cruel.

A few years later, Terry turned up again looking for more cash. He blackmailed the Hortons, 'reselling' Tommy to them for £10,000 – which was the final straw for poor Vera. She tore up all

RIGHT: **Vera Duckworth is surprised to win a car in a "Husband Of The Year" competition. Jack reveals he entered the competition under her name and is annoyed when Vera says she's keeping the car for herself!**

BELOW: **Vera is delighted to think she is a cousin of the Queen after Joss Shackleton, who claims to be Vera's biological dad, tells her he is the illegitimate son of King Edward VII!**

WOMAN'S CHOICE

ENTER OUR "HUSBAND OF THE YEAR" COMPETITION AND THIS LUXURY CAR COULD BE YOURS!

WIN THIS FABULOUS VAUXHALL NOVA 1.4 SR

To enter, fill out this entry form telling us in fifteen words or less why your husband deserves to be crowned **"HUSBAND OF THE YEAR"**. Send your completed entry form (no photocopies allowed) to **WOMAN'S CHOICE** at the address on page 4. Closing date for entries is **Monday 30th June 1986**. The lucky winner will be notified by post. The Judges' decision is final.

My Husband deserves to be crowned "Husband Of The Year" because *RIGHT FROM THE DAY WE WERE MARRIED HE HAS MADE MY LIFE ONE LONG HONEYMOON*

Name *VERA DUCKWORTH*

Address *9 CORONATION ST. WEATHERFIELD, MANCHESTER, GM1 5DC*

Daytime phone number *0161 715 2119*

Buckingham Palace
1st April 1991

We have been pleased to hear of our relationship with Mrs Vera Duckworth.

We earnestly hope however that this will be cognoscente of the delicate nature of the circumstance and of the necessity of keeping this information within, as it were, the family.

E. R.

BELOW: **A happy snap of Tyrone and Molly on their Big Day in 2009... but it isn't long before Molly begins an affair with Tyrone's work mate Kevin Webster.**

To my darling Husband,
I will love you forever,
M.
xxx

Street for ever in February 1989 – was the arrival of her stone cladding. She loved it and was extremely upset no-one else seemed to share her excitement.

Always on the lookout for a scam, Jack once entered a contest in one of Vera's magazines.

Ironically, the object was to describe why he should win husband of the year, and Jack took some licence in writing, 'My husband is husband of the year because, right from the start, he has made my life one long honeymoon.'

It won the competition, but as he had entered in Vera's name, she claimed the prize: a sparkling new Vauxhall Nova. As she couldn't drive, Jack expected Vera to hand the car over to him, but a determined Vera signed up for lessons and passed her test.

The years of scrimping and scraping finally ended for the Duckworths when they received an even bigger windfall from Jack's brother Cliff, who left him £30,000 after dying in a car accident in Spain.

Hearing that the Rovers was still up for grabs, Jack and Vera jumped at the chance to own their local boozer. But the eager couple faced stiff competition from Jim and Liz McDonald, and the race for the Rovers was on. When the Duckworths raised the asking price by selling No.9 to Gary and Judy Mallett, the pub where Jack had spent years working as a cellarman finally became theirs – and although their tenure may have been brief, the Duckworths had finally moved up in the world.

After selling the Rovers in 1998, Jack and Vera managed Eunice Gee's B&B, before buying back their old home at No.9. Vera took on a part-time job at Roy's Rolls – her own brand of gobby customer service never failing to surprise owner Roy – but decided to retire for good in 2007.

Vera started to dream of a new life by the seaside in Blackpool at around the time of their golden wedding anniversary. However, a fresh start by the sea was not to be for Jack and Vera. Back home, after a day in Blackpool planning their move, Vera flopped into her armchair, asked Jack to fetch her slippers and told him that she loved him. Jack grudgingly reciprocated, before heading to the pub for a much-needed pint. Later, he returned to find Vera dozing where he'd left her but, on trying to wake her, realised that Vera had died in her sleep. Jack held his beloved Vera for the very last time before breaking the news to

> **Burglars? Your house? Anything worth pinching they'd have to bring with 'em.**
>
> ALEC GILROY COMFORTING
> THE DUCKWORTHS

LEFT: **Gary Mallett hands the keys of No.9 back to the Duckworths**

BELOW, LEFT: **Tyrone becomes one of the family**

BELOW: **Molly tries to take down the stone cladding**

anyone. Vera Duckworth was as much a part of Coronation Street as the cobbles themselves and, as the residents attending her packed funeral sagely agreed, Weatherfield would never see her like again.

ABOVE: **Jack prepares to say goodbye to his 'Vee'**
RIGHT: **Molly leaves Tyrone**

Nobody could replace Vera in Jack's heart, but he did find companionship with Connie Rathbone. As well as both being recently widowed, they bonded over their mutual love of pigeons, which was music to Jack's ears after all the years of Vera calling them 'vermin'. Tyrone thought Connie was a gold-digger, but it turned out that she was the one with the money, as Jack discovered when he moved in to her mansion.

Tyrone and Molly bought No.9 from Jack. In January 2009, they got married in a fairy-tale ceremony, marred only by Tyrone's dreadful mother, Jackie, stealing their honeymoon flight tickets.

While Tyrone lapped up married life, Molly became increasingly restless. All the things she

> ‘ **I can just see our Vera in a hard hat. It would go with her hard face, wouldn't it?** ’
>
> JACK

> You all knew Jack. He loved a pint, he loved a bet, he loved his pigeons. But most of all he loved Vera.
>
> TYRONE AT JACK'S FUNERAL

ABOVE: **Jack is forced to kiss and make up** BELOW: **Molly in bed with Kevin Webster**

had once liked about him suddenly became a turn-off, not least his habit of sitting at the dinner table in his stained vest. She caught the eye of Kevin Webster and they went running together. Soon they were doing laps around hotel bedrooms. Kevin promised Molly that he would leave Sally, but the latter's illness put paid to that, and even when Molly discovered she was pregnant, Kevin refused to change his mind. Heartbroken Molly stayed with Tyrone and allowed him to believe she was expecting his baby.

Two years after the death of his wife Vera, Jack Duckworth discovered he had non-Hodgkin's lymphoma and just a few weeks left to live. Tyrone

was devastated by the news but arranged a big 74th birthday party for Jack in the Rovers, knowing it would be the last hurrah for the man who was like a father to him. Later that evening, Jack returned home to No.9 and quietly passed away in the same armchair as Vera. In his final moments, Jack had a vision of Vera. The couple danced together, and Vera warned her hubby he had better hurry up because they needed to catch the bus 'at 12 minutes past. So shift yourself!'

Molly gave birth to a boy, who she and Tyrone named Jack in a touching tribute. Tyrone was overjoyed to finally have a family of his own, but ultimately, Molly realized she was still in love with Kevin and abandoned her marriage, leaving Tyrone bruised and bewildered. He had always hoped that they would be married for as long as Jack and Vera; instead they had barely made it past their first anniversary. With Kevin still unwilling to choose her over his family, heartbroken Molly decided to leave Weatherfield with Jack. But just as Molly was saying goodbye to former co-worker Sunita Alahan at the Corner Shop, a gas explosion at The Joinery bar caused a tram to derail and crash down into the shop, trapping Molly, Jack and Sunita in the wreckage. Sunita and Jack were

Kirsty hit it off for real, but Tyrone was unaware Kirsty had a dangerous and violent temper. She first attacked him with a ladle in the kitchen at No.9 and later crushed his arm in a door. When Kirsty discovered she was pregnant, Tyrone couldn't bring himself to leave her and suffered in silence. When Tommy, new lodger Tina McIntyre and Tyrone's ex-girlfriend Fiz Stape began to notice what was going on, they all found themselves targeted by twisted Kirsty, who warned them nobody would come between her and Tyrone. After giving birth to their daughter Ruby, in the Rovers, Kirsty and Tyrone's relationship completely unravelled and she vengefully framed him for assault, resulting in Tyrone's arrest. But during Tyrone's trial, Kirsty broke down, admitted she needed help and gave him custody of Ruby.

Tyrone's nightmare with Kirsty brought him and Fiz back together, and they have lived (mostly) happily together at No.9 since 2013 with his daughter, Ruby, and her daughter, Hope. Apart from the occasional unexpected house guest, one-night stand, car crash and life-or-death medical emergency, that is.

both rescued, but Molly was badly injured and didn't survive. On the day of Molly's funeral, Tyrone finally discovered the truth. As it sank in that his wife had given birth to his best mate's baby, Tyrone flipped, punched Kevin and sent him tumbling into Molly's open grave.

After all that, Tyrone lost his way with women. So his lodger, Tommy Duckworth, secretly paid a woman, Kirsty Soames, to flirt with Tyrone at a bar to boost his confidence. Tommy's meddling more than paid off when Tyrone and policewoman

ABOVE: **In 2012 Tyrone becomes a victim of domestic violence at the hands of girlfriend Kirsty** BELOW: **At Christmas 2015 Tyrone transforms the Street into Lapland for Fiz's sick daughter Hope after she is diagnosed with a rare form of cancer**

The vamp that lights up the Street

№ 11 CORONATION ST.

RESIDENTS

1960–1984
ELSIE & DENNIS TANNER

1970–1973
ALAN HOWARD

1974–1976
KEN & JANET BARLOW

1976–1979
GAIL POTTER & SUZIE BIRCHALL

1984–1985
BILL, KEVIN & DEBBIE WEBSTER

1985
HARRY, CONNIE, ANDREA & SUE CLAYTON

1986–1989
ALF & AUDREY ROBERTS

1989–2000
JIM, LIZ, STEVE & ANDY McDONALD

2001–PRESENT
EILEEN GRIMSHAW

2004–2016
SEAN TULLY

2005–2007
VIOLET WILSON

2010–2012
ROSIE WEBSTER

2001–2016
JASON GRIMSHAW

2001–2004, 2013–2017
TODD GRIMSHAW

2015
MICHAEL RODWELL

2016–2018
PAT PHELAN

2017–PRESENT
SEB & ABI FRANKLIN

2018
NICOLA RUBINSTEIN

The deep-red lipstick, the film-star hair, the big collars, the 'come hither hand on hip' – Elsie Tanner was the Street's siren for over 20 years, with a seemingly endless queue of men ready to take her out and show her a good time. Typically following her heart instead of her head, the results would often be traumatic thanks to the type of men she chose. Usual relationship terminators were their violent tempers, drink problems or, most likely, their wives.

In her time, the glamorous divorcee turned her hand to almost anything to pay the bills – shop assistant, model, croupier, florist, receptionist and supervisor at Mike Baldwin's factory – unlike her drifter son Dennis, who couldn't hold down any job and was forever nicking two bob from his mum's purse. However, daughter Linda

> **For years and years I have shut my eyes and ears to the goings-on at No.11 Coronation Street...**
>
> ENA SHARPLES

BELOW: **Mum's the word. Elsie reminds son Dennis who is boss in 1961**

was much more like her mother – a strong-minded and feisty girl who liked to get her own way.

In 1967, Elsie married American Steve Tanner, who had fallen for Elsie during the war. But after their much heralded new start in the States, Elsie returned home to Weatherfield thanks to Steve's drinking and violence towards her. Her husband soon followed, but was found dead at the foot of a flight of stairs in a saga that saw a variety of the locals – even Elsie – suspected of his murder. It turned out he'd been killed during a fight over a debt.

RIGHT: **Elsie with the only two real loves of her life – Dennis and Len** BELOW, RIGHT: **Still turning heads in 1978** LEFT: **Elsie and Ena at each other's throats** BELOW, LEFT: **Breakfast at No.11 for Elsie and daughter Linda**

Elsie Tanner's heart is where a fella's wallet is – and the bigger the wallet, the more heart she's got.

HILDA OGDEN

Two years later, Elsie tied the knot with husband number three, garage owner Alan Howard, but things weren't to work out. Yet again, he turned out to be a boozer who drank away any money he earned.

In many ways, Elsie's longest relationship was probably her 20-years of (almost) marriage to Len Fairclough. They'd had a passionate but brief affair in the early sixties and had looked out for each other ever since. In her later days in Weatherfield, Elsie described him as, 'The only man who ever truly loved me.'

Elsie's other life-spanning relationship was the long-running feud with her no-nonsense busybody neighbour Ena Sharples. Neither of them flinched from speaking their minds, but the pair couldn't have been more opposite. Floozy Elsie with her cheap, busty glamour; and Ena, religious and disapproving, with her hairnets and scrubbed face.

When Elsie received a poison-pen letter questioning her morals in 1961, she was convinced that Ena had written it. She snarled, 'That woman's tongue – if it was a bit longer she could shave with it.' Elsie confronted Ena in the Street, resulting in the pair ranting at each other while the residents looked on. But the next day, she received a card from her ex-husband Arnold, apologising for the letter sent by his jealous new girlfriend Norah.

Although their rows continued, it was clear in later years that these very different women had begun to respect and soften towards each other.

By the early eighties, Elsie was back working at Baldwin's Casuals as a lowly machinist and the future was not looking especially bright for the ageing glamour puss. Life seemed to have come to a dead end. But then old flame Bill Gregory reappeared in Weatherfield – they'd had an affair over 20 years earlier – and he whisked her off to the sunny Algarve where he ran a wine bar. After years of disappointment with men, finally Elsie had a fresh start to smile about.

If Elsie's relationships were difficult, then Jim and Liz McDonald's marriage was positively stormy. In 1989, mum-of-two Liz, after years of moving around army bases, was determined to make No.11 their first real home, but ex-army man Jim never quite got used to civilian life. And when their baby daughter Katie died when she was just a day old, it made the tension between them even more difficult.

Ultimately, Jim's violent temper led to the end of their marriage. When Liz told him she'd slept with one of his best friends during their army days, he flipped, hit her, and they eventually divorced.

If sensible student Andy was the golden boy of the family, then his twin brother Steve was most definitely the black sheep. Despite being in love with hairdresser Fiona Middleton, he married rich heiress Vicky Arden – Alec Gilroy's granddaughter – for no other reason than to pay off his debts to loan sharks and enjoy the high life. But in recent years, after a spell inside for dodgy dealings, Steve's law-breaking days are well and truly behind him.

When feisty Karen Phillips first arrived on Coronation Street in 2000, the locals had no idea what was about to hit them – often quite literally. She was given a job at Underworld by her old school friend Linda Sykes and married Steve for a bet, yet somehow their marriage worked. She loved him, but not enough for her to resist temptation when it arrived in the form of Joe Carter, Mike's new sidekick at the factory.

The younger McDonalds separated and, while they were apart, Steve had a one-night stand with Tracy Barlow, the woman who was to become Karen's nemesis. Eventually, Karen fell into Joe's arms, but then came the shocking realisation that he had just been using her to help pull a scam over Mike at the factory. Humiliated, Karen fled to her aunt's, until Steve tracked her down and forgave her.

They decided to go through with their divorce so they could marry again in style and renew their vows. Despite all the planning, the day was rocked by the arrival of Tracy, announcing that it was Steve who was baby Amy's real father and ruining what was meant to be the best day of Karen's life. The couple still married, but after the emotional upheaval of losing her own baby, Karen unintentionally put Amy's life in danger and Steve threw her out. She left alone on Christmas Day 2004.

> ' Half the street think
> you're a slag.
> The other half think
> you're a nutter.
> I think you're both! '
>
> STEVE McDONALD TO
> HIS WIFE KAREN

Currently holding the deeds to No.11 is salt-of-the-earth Eileen Grimshaw, cab controller at Street Cars, a woman who seems to be forever unlucky in love. First of all, biker Dennis Stringer left her for Janice Battersby, the ultimate slap in the face for any woman. Then, seemingly mild-mannered Ed Jackson turned out to be Ernest Bishop's killer, cheeky salesman Pat Stanaway had six other women on the go at the same time, and children's entertainer Jesse lavished more attention on his pet parrot than poor old Eileen, so he had to go. Like Elsie Tanner before her, when Eileen was in full cry, there was only room for one squawking bird in the house. Over the years, Eileen struggled to bring up her two sons on her own: Jason, the brawny builder and ladies' man,

and Todd, who after much heartache, confronted his own feelings and finally acknowledged he was gay after falling for nurse Karl.

Overall, 2004 was a life-changing year for Todd – especially when his girlfriend, Sarah Platt, lost their baby, Billy, who was born prematurely. It was a distressing time for both families and, while Sarah and Todd struggled to deal with their loss, their mothers, Eileen and Gail, continued the local tradition of slanging matches in the Street, hurling abuse and blame at each other for the tragedy.

Unlike Elsie and Ena's public displays of antipathy 40 years before, Gail and Eileen's mutual dislike for each other can lead to hair pulling and right hooks. All the same, in

69

ABOVE LEFT: **The happiest day of their lives? Steve and Karen's nuptials in 2004** LEFT: **Bride Karen lashes out at arch-enemy Tracy** ABOVE: **Jason and Eileen welcome Violet to No.11**

BELOW: **Elsie Tanner packs her bags and leaves Weatherfield for a new life in the USA after falling in love with American serviceman Steve Tanner.**

BELOW AND OPPOSITE: **Man magnet Elsie ruffles a few feathers during her years on the Street. In 1961 she assumes this poison pen letter is from her busybody neighbour Ena Sharples. But the culprit turns out to be someone quite unexpected!**

Dear Mrs Tanner,
IT IS QUITE OBVIOUS THAT YOU DO NOT KNOW THE LAW OF THE LAND, FOR IF YOU DID YOU WOULD KNOW THAT YOU ARE NOT ALLOWED TO GO MESSING ABOUT WITH MEN UNTIL YOU ARE ABSOLUTLY DIVORCED.

CERTAIN PEOPLE WOULD LIKE TO KNOW WHAT HAPPENED IN BLACKPOOL ILUMINATIONS BETWEEN YOU AND A CERTAIN GENTLMAN WHO WEARS A UNIFORM AND THIS INFORMATION WILL BE PASSED ON IF YOU DO NOT PUT YOUR HOUSE UP IN ORDER.

THIS IS A WARNING IF YOU THINK I DONT KNOW WHAT

I AM TALKING ABOUT YOU'V
ANOTHER THING COMING.

Weatherfield, when it comes to washing your dirty laundry in public, it looks like some things never change.

The feud was further fuelled by Jason's marriage to Sarah, which ended when he declined to join her in Italy. While waiting for his divorce from Sarah, he proposed to Becky Granger dressed in full naval costume – like Richard Gere in *An Officer and a Gentleman*. Given the effort Jason had made, he was understandably dismayed when she chose Steve McDonald instead. Although women always caused him grief, Jason remained an incurable romantic and was soon buying more engagement rings – for Tina McIntyre and then Eva Price. Despite this, Jason never married again before leaving Coronation Street for a life of foreign travel in 2016, much to the disappointment of Weatherfield's jewellers.

Being the mum of two troublesome sons has never made Eileen's life easy. Even when they weren't living under her roof, the pair still managed to leave Eileen shame-faced over their bad behaviour. Todd was a changed man when he moved back to Weatherfield from London in 2013, but not for the better. He seduced Maria Connor's boyfriend Marcus Dent, destroyed Eileen's quest for happiness with a new man she met online, and got into illegal dealings with Jason's dad Tony Stewart.

Eileen took in all manner of waifs and

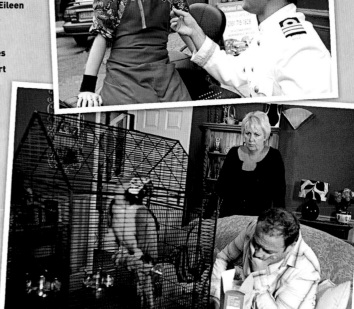

strays, but an unwelcome visitor was her father Colin, who she learned had impregnated her best friend Paula Carp when she was 14. This meant that Eileen and Paula's daughter Julie were half-sisters. Chalk and cheese doesn't begin to describe it. Eileen reluctantly allowed her father to stay but, just as he was about to be arrested for his crime, he died.

Eileen continued her unlucky streak when it came to picking men but didn't do herself any favours when she took a fancy to Gail's estranged husband Michael Rodwell, reigniting their feud and culminating in another dust-up in the street.

But Eileen's biggest romantic disaster by far was her marriage to Pat Phelan in 2017. Eileen soon learned that Pat wasn't averse to bending the rules when it came to business and she was furious to discover he had ripped off her friends and neighbours in a luxury apartments scam. Yet Pat's seemingly genuine love for her made Eileen blind to an even darker side to his nature and while away at a coastal cottage holiday in 2018, Eileen finally discovered the terrifying truth about the man she had married. During a

showdown at the foot of a lighthouse, Pat confessed to killing his dodgy property developer partner Vinny Ashford, local lads Andy Carver – whom he'd held prisoner in a cellar for months – and Luke Britton, and watching Michael Rodwell die from a heart attack. Before he could claim her as his next victim, Eileen pushed her husband, and he fell to his death in the sea.

But Pat was not a man to be easily got rid of, and a few months later, armed with a gun, he went on a rampage of revenge on the Street, shooting his daughter Nicola Rubinstein and Michelle Connor. Both women survived but the same could not be said for Pat, who perished at the hands of his long-standing enemy Anna Windass.

No doubt Eileen has sworn off men for the moment. But then again, she wouldn't be the first woman in Weatherfield to marry a murderer and then go on to pick another wrong 'un...and another and another.

24hr **S** service

STREET CARS

0161 715 1515

Airport trips, party bookings, weddings. Fast, reliable and safe

STREET CARS

All drivers are very friendly and polite
Most areas are covered/Weatherfield, Urmston, Stretford, etc.
Special rates to the airports
If you are unhappy with our service or feel that you have been
overcharged, please contact the office as soon as possible.

RECEIPT

From CORONATION ST. To AIRPORT

Date 13-MARCH-05 Drivers No 7684

Received (with thanks) £ 15.00

ABOVE: **Who's booked a cab?
It's crafty Cilla Brown and
boyfriend Les Battersby, who
sneak off for a holiday and
dump Cilla's poor son
Chesney on the neighbours!**

RIGHT: **Invitation to Steve
and Karen's doomed
second wedding, which is
gatecrashed by Steve's
ex-fling Tracy Barlow
who reveals Steve got her
pregnant while he and
Karen were separated!**

*Elizabeth McDonald
Requests
the pleasure of
Mrs Eileen Grimshaw*

*on the occasion of the
wedding reception of her Son
Steven McDonald
with
Karen McDonald
Niece of Eva Briggs
on
Sunday 15th February 2004
at
Walcot Manor at 3pm*

RSVP   Dress Code:Smart Casual

BELOW: **Andy Carver sends out a desperate SOS when he's held captive in the basement of an abandoned house by serial killer Pat Phelan in 2017.**

MY NAME IS ANDY CARVER,

PAT PHELAN HAS ME HOSTAGE IN

A CELLAR, NEAR TRAIN TRACK.

INFORM POLICE.

Unlucky for some – especially Hilda

№13 CORONATION ST.

RESIDENTS

1960–1962
MAY & CHRISTINE HARDMAN

1963–1964
JERRY & MYRA BOOTH

1964–1987
STAN, HILDA & IRMA OGDEN

1980–1983
EDDIE YEATS

1986–2008
KEVIN, SALLY, ROSIE & SOPHIE WEBSTER

2008–2010
ASHLEY, CLAIRE, JOSHUA & FREDDIE PEACOCK

2011
LLOYD MULLANEY

2011
CHERYL, RUSS & CHRIS GRAY

2012
STEVE & TRACY MCDONALD AND AMY BARLOW

2012
BETH & CRAIG TINKER

2012–2013, 2014–PRESENT
KEVIN & JACK WEBSTER

2013–2014
STELLA, GLORIA & EVA PRICE

2014–2016, 2018–PRESENT
SOPHIE WEBSTER

2014–2015
MADDIE HEATH

2016–2017
ANNA & FAYE WINDASS

76

When the Ogdens entered a Mr & Mrs contest at the Rovers, they failed to get any of the questions right, which pretty much sums up their marriage. It may be one of the longest in Street history, but the pair couldn't have been more different. Hilda was permanently on the go – whether cleaning and gossiping at the Rovers and Dr Lowther's, or bickering with Stan, she was a woman who just could not sit still. She had an opinion on everything and everyone, and no-one was safe from her tongue-lashings or the sound of her birdlike, high-pitched singing.

However, if sitting still was an Olympic event, Stan would have won a gold medal. While Hilda would scurry from job to job in order to pay the bills, ever-skiving Stan would rarely shift his weight from his armchair. Not a great conversationalist, he was happiest supping a pint in the Rovers and staring into space.

As a result of regular ear-bashings from Hilda, Stan would attempt to find work, but he drifted from job to job. In the early sixties his occupations included ice-cream salesman, milkman, chauffeur and photographer. He even tried professional wrestling, but only managed one match, during which he was thrown from the ring into Hilda's lap. However, in 1969 Stan bought a window-cleaning round and he stuck with the profession for the rest of his life – mainly because in between

ABOVE: **Psychic Hilda reads the tea leaves in 1969**
BELOW: **Hilda reminds henpecked Stan that she's the one who wears the trousers, 1970**

appointments he could pop into his beloved Rovers for a pint.

The Ogdens may never have had any money, but Hilda took great pride in her house. With her scenic 'murial' of the Canadian Rockies, complete with flying ducks, she thought it the epitome of style and taste. Hilda was forever keeping up with the Joneses too. When she found out Betty Turpin had just had a shower installed, she had to have one too. But when Len told her it would

be too expensive, she opted for a serving hatch instead – which she adored.

They say 13 is an unlucky number, and the Ogdens certainly never had much luck, especially when it came to money. In 1966 Stan thought he'd won the pools, but Hilda had just used the coupon to fill in the winning numbers. When Hilda broke the bad news to him, he went berserk and tried to strangle her – probably using more energy in those few minutes than he had in a lifetime.

At one point, Hilda was even thinking about becoming a professional clairvoyant, but that didn't work out either, as nothing she predicted came true. The couple had a colour television delivered, but it was quickly repossessed. And then, in 1973, in a rare moment of generosity, Stan promised to take Hilda anywhere she liked for her birthday. Hilda chose a day in Paris – but in true Ogden style they missed the plane, spent the day at the airport and pretended that they did actually go.

However, during their lifetime of disappointment, occasionally good fortune came knocking on the door of No.13. In 1971, they won £500 on the premium bonds, and after they'd paid off their debts, the pair went on a shopping spree with the leftover £95. In a bid to go upmarket, they bought a coffee percolator, a tray, a cocktail bar and an electric toothbrush. Five years later, Hilda won another competition – a trolley dash at a delicatessen. But minutes before the start, very

conveniently, Stan put his back out, so Deirdre Langton had to stand in and race around the store in two minutes with Hilda. In the end, the shop owner agreed to give them £75 and some caviar instead of the goods, and that night – for the first and last time – the Ogdens settled down to a dinner of caviar and chips.

By 1977, Hilda was fed up with their never-ending run of bad luck and told Stan she wanted their house number changed. For her birthday, he replaced the sign on the door with 12a. But while Stan proudly showed Hilda their new lucky house number, they got locked out, their roast lamb burnt, and Stan had to smash a window to get the spare key.

Eventually, the Ogdens actually won something they could use in a 'Loving Cup Shandies' competition, with Hilda's third-prize-winning slogan 'Be a mistress as well as a wife and your husband'll still be a boyfriend'. The prize was a second honeymoon night in a five-star hotel with £25 spending money. Stan didn't want to go and suggested that Hilda went on her own, an idea

that, unsurprisingly, went down like a lead balloon. She told him he was going, even if she had to chain him to her.

So, with a negligee borrowed from Rita in the suitcase, the Ogdens set off for their second honeymoon. At the hotel, Hilda couldn't stop admiring the luxurious room, while Stan couldn't keep his eyes off the minibar – and the huge colour television. After a bottle of complimentary champagne to get them in the mood, Hilda had romantic plans for the night, but not only was Stan soon out for the count, he was snoring loudly too.

He may have driven her to distraction, but Hilda couldn't imagine life without Stan. When he died in his sleep following a long illness in 1984, just after they'd celebrated their ruby wedding anniversary, she was bereft. As she unpacked Stan's bag, Hilda's brave face finally betrayed her, and she broke down in tears.

The following year, she took in young mechanic Kevin as a lodger, and he became like a son to her, with Hilda becoming as overprotective as any real mother. When Kevin started dating Sally Seddon,

77

ABOVE: **Stan prepares to celebrate their wedding anniversary in 1968** FAR LEFT: **All smiles for the unlucky Ogdens** LEFT: **Fish & chips with lodger Eddie Yeats, 1981** BELOW: **Hilda keeps a watchful eye over Kevin and Sally in 1986**

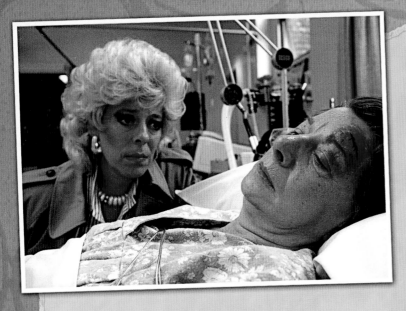

LEFT: **A worried Bet visits Hilda in hospital after she is mugged**

BELOW: **Sally reveals her breast cancer diagnosis to Kevin at Christmas 2009**

What, us? Buy a telly? I've got more chance of a proposal from Michael Heseltine...

HILDA FEELING DESPONDENT

she hit the roof, saying the Seddon family were as rough as they come. She began to monitor the young couple's every move and wouldn't allow any 'funny business' under her roof. When Hilda began to suspect that Sally was spending the night, she even laid a wire trap on the stairs, but she forgot about it and fell down the stairs herself, spraining her ankle. Unable to work with her injury, she was forced to ask Sally to stand in for her.

As time passed, Hilda became fond of Sally and duly sobbed into her hanky at the Websters' wedding in 1986. When Hilda left Weatherfield to become live-in housekeeper at Dr Lowther's countryside home just after Christmas in 1987, she sold the house to the couple for a bargain price. She'd just been mugged and told Sally she'd be taking the good memories with her and leaving the bad ones behind, and she wanted to give the Websters an

easier start in life than hers had been. On her final night in Weatherfield, Hilda was touched when the residents threw her a farewell party at the Rovers, where she'd worked as a cleaner for 20 years – driving first lady Annie Walker mad for much of that time. She was presented with heated rollers by Bet and led everyone in a rendition of "Wish Me Luck As You Wave Me Goodbye", Coronation Street echoing to the sound of Hilda's shrill yet comforting tones for the very last time.

In 2008, the Peacocks of No. 4 swapped houses with the Websters, enabling Sally – or 'Lady Webster' as Janice Battersby sneeringly called her – to acquire a residence more in keeping with her social status. A new house brought the same old problems, however, with daughters Rosie and Sophie at each other's throats. While Sophie turned to God, Rosie's idea of a deity was Katie Price. After Rosie had been kidnapped by John Stape, Sophie felt so ignored by the rest of the family that she sent a postcard threatening that her own life was in danger just to get some attention.

Of course, Rosie soon bounced back from her ordeal and sank her claws into her new boss at Underworld, Luke Strong. Armed with £150,000 guilt money from John, she bought shares in Underworld, but was horrified when Luke later ran off with her fortune. At last, Rosie had met someone shallower than her.

Meanwhile, Kevin had been conducting a steamy affair with Molly Dobbs, but that ended when Sally was diagnosed with breast cancer. Kevin realised that he couldn't leave Sally in her hour of need. His place was at her side, with his family, for better or worse.

There are lots of superstitious folk down Weatherfield way who think No.13 is cursed. Indeed, the Peacock family was doomed when dad Ashley was killed in a gas explosion at The Joinery bar in December 2010. The same explosion caused a tram to derail and crash onto the Street, causing No.13 to go up in flames and leaving Ashley's widow Claire and their two sons, Joshua and Freddie, temporarily homeless.

When Street Cars co-owner Lloyd Mullaney purchased the property the following year to live in with his girlfriend Cheryl Gray and her young son Russ, he hoped he'd be the one to avoid the curse. No such luck! The kind-hearted cabbie made the mistake of letting Cheryl's estranged husband Chris move into the house after he was diagnosed with a brain tumour. However, Lloyd was unaware Chris's condition was not as critical as he claimed. Crafty Chris continued to lie and used the living arrangements to woo back wife Cheryl, leaving poor Lloyd heartbroken.

The house got a dodgy DIY makeover when Lloyd's business partner, Steve McDonald, bought the place in 2012. Steve's short-lived marriage to Tracy Barlow was already on its last legs, so Steve converted the house into two separate flats so he wouldn't have to see his hated wife. To Tracy's horror, Steve also let his former girlfriend Beth Tinker, her teenage son Craig and his pet rat Darryl move in. Factory machinist Beth couldn't stand Tracy initally, so things were far from harmonious between the housemates from hell until their proximity resulted in their forming an enduring relationship.

Kevin Webster returned to his roots and is No. 13's current resident, living there with his son Jack and daughter Sophie. But since his marriage break-up with Sally, garage owner Kevin has continued to be unlucky in love. He dated old friend Jenny Bradley in 2015, but Jenny was a troubled soul. Having lost her own son Tom in a drowning accident years earlier, Jenny became obsessed with Jack, snatched him and did a runner. When Kevin, Sophie and family friend Rita Tanner tracked her down, they found Jenny holding Jack dangerously close to the edge of an apartment balcony. Jenny was later sectioned under the Mental Health Act.

Kevin's relationship with Anna Windass looked like it could be the real deal when she and teenage daughter Faye moved in. Unfortunately, Anna was caught in a nasty feud with Pat Phelan, the local builder who had menaced her family and blackmailed Anna into sleeping with him. Phelan soon began to target Kevin too, and tried to sabotage Kevin's garage business.

ABOVE LEFT: **Rosie with Luke Strong** ABOVE MIDDLE: **Rosie being held hostage by John Stape** ABOVE RIGHT: **Rosie as a roller-skating vodka promotions girl**
BELOW RIGHT: **There's high drama when Kevin's girlfriend Jenny snatches his young son Jack in 2015**
BELOW: **Jason saves Simon when No.13 catches fire during the 2010 tram crash**

When Anna was framed by Phelan for a crime she didn't commit, Kevin decided that the constant drama was unsettling for seven-year-old Jack and called time on their relationship. Heartbroken Anna was sent to prison for five years, but secured an early release when Phelan's catalogue of crimes came to light, and returned to Weatherfield to get even with the man who'd made her family's lives a misery for years. A desperate Phelan had gate-crashed Michelle and Robert's wedding ceremony at the Bistro and taken bride Michelle hostage. However the tables were finally turned when Anna confronted her rapist in the restaurant's kitchen and plunged a knife into his chest. Anna watched as Phelan gasped his last breath, and the residents agreed to cover up Anna's crime, claiming she killed Phelan in self-defence. With her bloody work done, Anna decided to leave Weatherfield for a new life in Durham. Meanwhile, Kevin put his love life on hold when Jack devastatingly contracted sepsis and, to prevent the infection spreading, had his foot amputated. But with his family rallying round, Kevin has been a tower of strength to young Jack, as he adjusts to his daily challenges with a commendable attitude of positivity.

RIGHT: **In 1966, Stan thinks he's won a fortune on the pools. But when wife Hida breaks the bad news he hasn't, he snaps and tries to strangle her!**

RIGHT: **Kevin and Sally are married for over a decade until his affair with his business partner Natalie Horrocks and her relationship with the abusive Greg Kelly ruins everything.**

NO: 4556735

Matrimonial cause proceeding in the Principal Registry **treated by virtue of section 42 of** the Matrimonial and **Family Proceedings Act 1984** as pending and current **county court**

BETWEEN	MR KEVIN JOHN WEBSTER	Petitioner
AND	MRS SALLY WEBSTER	Respondent

Referring to the decree made in this cause on the 19.7.1999 whereby it was decree on the marriage solemnised on the 8.10.1986

at REGISTER OFFICE the District of WEATHERFIELD in the Metropolitan Borough SALFORD
between MR WEBSTER the Petitioner

and MRS WEBSTER the Respondent

be dissolved unless sufficient cause be shown to the Court why the said decree should not be made absolute, and no such cause having been shown, it is hereby certified that the said decree was on the 3.9.1999 made final and absolute and that the said marriage was thereby dissolved. The period of six weeks having been reduced by Judges order of the said decree.

Notes:

1. Divorce affects inheritance under a will
   Where a will has already been made by either party to the marriage then, by virtue Wills Act 1837:
   (a) any provisions of the will appointing the former spouse executor or trustee or conferr appointment on the former spouse shall take effect as if the former spouse had died on the ate on which the marriage is dissolved unless a contrary intention appears in the will;

   (b) any property which, or an interest in which, is devised or bequeathed to the former as if the former spouse had died on the date on which the marriage is dissolved unless appears in the will.

2. Divorce affects the appointment of a guardian

   Unless a contrary intention is shown in the instrument of appointment, any appointment or 5(4) of the Children Act 1989 by one spouse of his or her former spouse as guardian section 6 of that Act, deemed to have been revoked at the date of the dissolution of the marriage

Signature of Petitioner: K.J. Webster	Date: 3.9.99
Signature of Respondant: Sally Webster	Date: 3.9.99

Watermark Bank
ST JOHNS HOUSE
LONDON SW1 7UP

PO BOX 23
61 Cresent Road
Weatherfield GM2 4TH

02 - 01 - 79

Date 16/01/2005

Pay *Sally Webster*   only

To sum of *Two Thousand Five Hundred*

Pounds only

Account payee

£2500

This cheque contains 33% recycled paper

Mr Ian Davenport
DAVENPORTS PRESTIGE MOTORS

.:194442322.:   02:2000   1211443OO7O

82

RIGHT: **When Alf Roberts decides to stand in the local elections in 1991, his chances are almost scuppered by an unfortunate spelling mistake on his campaign posters!**

VOTE
ALF ROBERTS

THE PEOPLE'S FIEND

Groceries and gossip on the corner

THE CORNER SHOP

PROPRIETORS

1960–1965
FLORRIE LINDLEY

1965–1966
LIONEL & SANDRA PETTY

1966–1968
DAVID & IRMA BARLOW

1968–1974
LES, MAGGIE & GORDON CLEGG

1974–1975
GRANNY, IDRIS & VERA HOPKINS

1976–1994
ALF, RENEE & AUDREY ROBERTS

1993
BRENDAN SCOTT

1994–1997
REG & MAUREEN HOLDSWORTH

1997–1999
FRED ELLIOTT

1999
RAVI, VIK & NITA DESAI

1999–PRESENT
DEV ALAHAN

2004-2006, 2010–2013
SUNITA ALAHAN

Quite what Florrie Lindley would have made of Mad Maya's crazed shop-burning antics, not to mention her attempts to frame Sunita as a bigamist, is anyone's guess – life was a lot quieter when she took over the Corner Shop in 1960. Psychotic ex-girlfriends with a penchant for murder weren't really big in Weatherfield back then. In fact, the most shocking thing Florrie ever did was to be caught by the police selling firelighters after seven in the evening, for which she was rapped on the knuckles with a £1 fine.

At first, the shop didn't exactly do a roaring trade under Florrie's management, and she worried about paying her bills – mainly because her customers seemed in no hurry to settle theirs. To make matters worse, a new supermarket opened in Rosamund Street, and for a short time, trade went down as customers flocked there. Thankfully, Florrie's regular customers returned, as they realised a better deal was to be had on Coronation Street.

It soon became clear that Florrie was a lonely woman who craved a man more than a career in retail. Bizarrely, she'd lied to her customers that she was a widow, when in fact she was only estranged from her husband, Norman. In 1965, he tracked her down to Weatherfield and begged her to give their marriage another try. After a heart-to-heart with Elsie Tanner, Florrie decided Norman was worth it, and the couple were waved

ABOVE: **In the beginning. The corner shop's very first owner Florrie Lindley in 1960**
BELOW: **Elsie catches up on the gossip with the Cleggs in 1968** BELOW, LEFT: **David and Irma Barlow hold the fort**

HALF PRICE

84

> ## He'd skin a flea and then sell it in a vest, would Alf Roberts...
>
> **HILDA OGDEN**

off by the residents as they immigrated to Canada.

Unlike Florrie, the best-remembered owner of the Corner Shop, Alf Roberts, felt right at home behind the counter. Portly local councillor Alf was an old-fashioned yet kindly man, whose love of his shop outshone almost everything else in his life.

After his wife Phyllis died, Alf took early retirement from the GPO and had his first taste of Corner Shop life when he took a shine to the strong-willed new proprietor Renee Bradshaw. After wooing Renee with a combination of business acumen and brawn – by helping her with VAT and putting up new shelves in the shop – she finally agreed to marry him. The pair tied the knot at Weatherfield Registry Office in March 1978 and, like most Street weddings, the day wasn't uneventful. When Renee's resentful stepfather Joe congratulated him for marrying Renee for her money, Alf managed to bite his tongue. But when Joe then added that Renee was lucky to get married as she wasn't very attractive, Alf finally snapped and punched him to the ground.

Happily, the couple's bumpy start to married life was followed by two years of wedded bliss. But the Roberts' happiness was to be short-lived. In 1980, they decided to sell the Corner Shop and move to leafy Grange-over-Sands to run a post office. In preparation, Renee asked Alf to teach her to drive, and while out in the countryside, she stalled the car at some roadworks. As Alf got out of the car to take over the driving, a lorry came down the lane and hit the car head-on, with Renee still inside. She underwent emergency surgery but died during the operation. Alf was inconsolable – he felt lost without his beloved wife and blamed himself for letting her drive. All he could do was throw himself back into his other love – the shop.

Whereas Alf was at his happiest when wearing his white grocer's coat, shop work hardly held the same appeal for his social-climbing third wife, Gail's mum, Audrey Potter. Flighty Audrey was the complete opposite of sensible Alf, yet somehow

their marriage worked – her giddiness livened him up, while his stoicism calmed her down. But the Corner Shop was a little downmarket for Audrey, who also worried that working such long hours would affect her Alfie's health, and she finally persuaded him to sell up in 1993.

But Alf's retirement didn't last long. After the Corner Shop's unpopular new owner, Brendan Scott, had a heart attack, Alf couldn't resist buying back his beloved shop premises at auction, telling Audrey he simply couldn't cope without it. Alf remained behind the counter until 1994, when Audrey made him sell again – this time for good – to Bettabuy employee Reg Holdsworth. Reg's dizzy wife Maureen managed the shop on a day-to-day basis, with her wheelchair-bound mother – and Reg's nemesis – Maud taking prime position behind the till.

If the demands of a thriving business, not to mention a wife like Audrey, were not enough, Alf also managed to devote time to another passion – local politics. He became a councillor in 1967, but lost his seat 20 years later when ex-employee Deirdre Barlow decided to stand against him and won by just seven votes. Alf was devastated and, while the other residents attended a party at the Rovers, he suffered a heart attack at home. As he

ABOVE LEFT: **Shop talk with Renee and Ena in 1976**
ABOVE RIGHT: **Going up in the world: Mayor Roberts and his ball and chain in 1994**
LEFT: **Audrey tires of life in the corner shop**

SPECIAL OFFER

> 'This place is like the village of the damned. No-one seems remotely normal.'
>
> **SHOPKEEPER BRENDAN SCOTT**

recovered in hospital, he assured Deirdre he didn't blame her for what had happened, but Audrey wasn't quite so forgiving. In 1991, with Alec Gilroy as his campaign manager, Alf won back the seat – beating Deirdre by 1515 votes to 904, despite a glaring misprint on his campaign posters describing him as 'The People's Fiend'.

Becoming the local mayor was the icing on the cake for Alf, and although Audrey found council functions boring, she was in her element as Lady Mayoress – largely due to having a chauffeur-driven mayoral limo at her disposal. The only problem was she was using it for distinctly un-mayoral activities, such as shopping sprees. When Alf found out, he was furious, and a mortified Audrey was faced with the indignity of having to use the bus instead. She was even more humiliated when Alf sacked her for not performing her duties properly and asked Betty Turpin to be his Lady Mayoress instead.

When Alf's term in office ended, he was stunned to receive a letter from the Prime Minister offering him an OBE, and he duly went to Buckingham Palace to receive it. But Alf's health had never been his strong point, despite Audrey's

> 'He gets very absorbed in his food, does Alf, not to say covered in it.'
>
> **AUDREY**

ABOVE: **'Ooh me 'ead!' Shop assistant Deirdre offers Vera some pain relief in 1986** BELOW: **Charlie Stubbs rescues Sunita from the burning shop**

efforts to make him eat properly and take regular exercise. On New Year's Eve 1998, Alf died peacefully in his armchair after the stroke of midnight

The shop's current owner is ladies' man Dev Alahan, who has the dubious honour of having slept with both Tracy and Deirdre Barlow – something that didn't exactly endear him to poor old Ken. But it was shop assistant Sunita Alahan that became the love of Dev's life, a fact that didn't go down especially well with his bonkers ex-girlfriend Maya, who blamed sweet-hearted Sunita for her own split with Dev. So, as any sane person would do, she set Sunita up as part of an illegal immigrant scam, resulting in the bride-to-be being arrested and imprisoned on her wedding day. Even that wasn't enough revenge for the increasingly unhinged lawyer, whose next move was to set fire to the shop with both Sunita and Dev inside.

While the couple survived that ordeal, their

marriage didn't. When a pregnant Sunita discovered Dev had secret children by the women who ran his shops, she was unable to forgive him. After giving birth to twins, she left him in early 2006.

Dev has always seen himself as the epitome of cool, a view that was challenged when one of his many children, teenage daughter Amber, came to live with him. She viewed the ageing lothario as more of an embarrassment and wasn't afraid to tell him so. But Dev couldn't help himself and when his golfing partner Prem Mandal introduced him to his wife Nina – a man-hungry former Bollywood star – an affair inevitably followed. Dev did finally manage to extricate himself from Nina's clutches, but only because he had taken a shine to her daughter Tara.

Even by Dev's standards, this was a complex set-up and, in a way that only he could, he proceeded to make matters worse by having a one-night stand with solicitor Lisa Dalton during a brief break from Tara. When Tara found out, she publicly humiliated him at the opening of her art exhibition outside the Victoria Court flats. Dev saw it as the perfect opportunity to propose to her but, as he got down on one knee before a crowd of neighbours, she unveiled a huge photo of him stark naked – with the word 'LIAR' spray-painted in red across his privates. It was 'ta-ra' to Tara.

For all his womanising, Dev clung to the hope that he might one day win back Sunita, and so he was overjoyed in 2010 when she and the twins reappeared on the scene. But their reunion was far from smooth sailing. In December of that

86

year, a tram crashed off the viaduct and into Coronation Street, destroying the shop. Amidst the chaos while Sunita lay injured, Becky McDonald looted £5,000 of the shop's takings, which she needed to pay off her scheming half-sister Kylie Turner. To make matters worse, Dev had not insured the business and faced financial ruin, unable to afford the repairs. In desperation, Dev was forced to sell the other five convenience stores in his empire to stay afloat financially.

In the aftermath of Sunita's affair with Karl Munro in 2012, heartbroken Dev smashed up the shop and hit the bottle to drown his sorrows. Dev hoped to salvage their relationship but Sunita's death as a result of the Rovers' fire the following year left him a single father, running the shop alongside his other business interest, Prima Doner.

To this day, Dev continues to boost his bank balance by renting out 15a Coronation Street, the flat above the Corner Shop, which was where 13-year-old Faye Windass infamously gave birth to baby girl, Miley in 2015.

ABOVE: **Maud shows Maureen and Fred what she thinks of them** RIGHT, ABOVE: **Bettabuy boss Reg Holdsworth checks out the competition in 1990** RIGHT, BELOW: **Dev meets Tara Mandal.**
BELOW, LEFT: **Public humiliation for Dev.** BELOW, MIDDLE: **Faye's family is shocked when the school girl gives birth in 2015** BELOW, RIGHT: **In 2010 Molly and baby Jack are trapped when a tram de-rails and crashes into the shop!**

CERTIFIED COPY of an ENTRY OF MARRIAGE

Pursuant to the — Marriage Act 1960

MC 91002569

MRG/2001

Registration District *Weatherfield*

Marriage solemnized at *the Register Office* in the

District of *Weatherfield* in the *City of Manchester*

Date Married	Name and Surname	Age	Residence at time of marriage	Condition	Rank or profession	Fathers name , Rank or profession
Twenty Fifth October 2004	Devendra Alahan	40 years	3 Montreal House Weatherfield Quays	Bachelor	Shopkeeper	Ranjit Alahan, University Lecturer
	Sunita Pareth	26 years	3 Montreal House Weatherfield Quays	Spinster	Shop Assistant	Soresh Pareth, Bank Clerk

Married at *Weatherfield Register Office* by *S. V. Brooke*

This marriage was solemnized between us, *D. Alahan* / *S. Pareth* in the presence of us, *Hayley Cropper* / *Roy Cropper*

CERTIFIED AS AN ENTRY IN A REGISTER IN MY CUSTODY Registrar *S.V. Brooke*

~~Superintendent Registrar~~

Date *Twenty Fifth October 2004*

WARNING: THIS CERTIFICATE IS NOT EVIDENCE OF IDENTITY

88

CERTIFIED COPY of an ENTRY OF MARRIAGE

Pursuant to the — Marriage Act 1960

MC 91002492

MRG/2001

Registration District *Weatherfield*

Marriage solemnized at *the Register Office* in the

District of *Weatherfield* in the *City of Manchester*

Date Married	Name and Surname	Age	Residence at time of marriage	Condition	Rank or profession	Fathers name , Rank or profession
Twenty Seventh September 2004	Kostya Lazar	24 years	78 Hudel Street, Ordsall	Bachelor	Security Guard	Larson Lazar, Builder
	Sunita Parekh	26 years	15a Coronation Street, Weatherfield	Spinster	Shop Assistant	Soresh Parekh, Bank Clerk

Married at *Weatherfield Register Office* by *H. Barnes*

This marriage was solemnized between us, *K. Lazar* / *S. Parekh* in the presence of us, *Maria Lamle* / *Dominic Baker*

CERTIFIED AS AN ENTRY IN A REGISTER IN MY CUSTODY ~~Registrar~~

Deputy Superintendent Registrar *H. Barnes*

Date *Twenty Seventh September 2004*

WARNING: THIS CERTIFICATE IS NOT EVIDENCE OF IDENTITY

Sunita is arrested for bigamy on her and Dev's wedding day. It turns out Dev's jealous ex "Mad" Maya has married several illegal immigrants under Sunita's name and anonymously reported her love-rival to the authorities!

MC **91002478**

CERTIFIED COPY of an   ENTRY OF MARRIAGE
Pursuant to the   Marriage Act 1960

Registration District Weatherfield

MRG/2001

Marriage solemnized at __the Register Office_____ in the

District of __Weatherfield_____ in the City of Manchester

Date Married	Name and Surname	Age	Residence at time of marriage	Condition	Rank or profession	Fathers name , Rank or profession
Twenty First September 2004	Abdul Hamid	38 years	3a Temple Road, Whalley Range	Bachelor	Builder	Asif Hamid, Carpenter
	Sunita Parekh	26 years	15a Coronation Street, Weatherfield	Spinster	Shop Assistant	Soresh Parekh, Bank Clerk

Married at __Weatherfield Register Office_____ by J. Ratcliffe

This marriage was solemnized between us,   A. Hamid   in the presence of us,   Laurence Ball

   S. Parekh   Hannah Smith

CERTIFIED AS AN ENTRY IN A REGISTER IN MY CUSTODY   Registrar J. Ratcliffe

~~Superintendent Registrar~~

Date Twenty First September 2004

WARNING: THIS CERTIFICATE IS NOT EVIDENCE OF IDENTITY

Lady sings the Weatherfield news

It was in May 1973 that Rita Littlewood sold her very first newspaper, thanks to husband-to-be Len Fairclough, who bought the Rosamund Street shop, called it the Korner Kabin and installed her as its first manager. Whilst some may have found the switch from the glamour of Weatherfield's nightspots to red-eyed early starts in a paper shop hard to take, club singer Rita took to the life of a newsagent like a duck to water.

The Kabin is where Rita reigned as a pillar of the community, despite the attempt by 'compo'-seeking con artists Les Battersby and Cilla Brown to blacken her name in 2004. They falsely accused her of wounding little Chesney after she pushed him out of the shop when he refused to leave. After a defiant outburst in court protesting her innocence, Rita even spent a night in the cells. Despite the fact that her name was cleared, Rita was left shaken by the experience and vowed to sell her cherished Kabin. But it was Audrey Roberts who changed her mind, saying, 'Lovey, it's the world gone mad, not you.' Ever the survivor, Rita pulled herself together.

But it was not the first time the Kabin had brought heartache for Rita. In 1999, she was reunited with her former foster daughter, Sharon Gaskell, who was back in Weatherfield to get married. Rita loved having Sharon around, so when the big day ended in tears – the groom, Ian, was having an affair with Natalie Barnes – Rita was determined to keep Sharon in the Street, signing the Kabin over to her. But despite his extra-curricular activities, Sharon did eventually marry Ian. He then persuaded her to sell the Kabin and move away from Weatherfield. Poor Rita was forced to buy back her own shop for £40,000, with her faith in human nature severely dented.

A month after Rita's arrival at the Kabin, she employed Mavis Riley – who hiccupped through the whole of her interview. The pair were as chalk and cheese as they come, with straight-talking Rita often exasperated with Mavis's wittering and dithering, not to mention her attempts at writing romantic fiction.

In 1990, Rita transferred the shop to brand-new premises on Coronation Street itself, whilst she moved into the flat upstairs. Two years later, she fell in love with former toffee salesman Ted Sullivan and, despite knowing he had a brain tumour, married him and they had three happy months together before he died.

In 1997, it was time for Rita to say another emotional goodbye when Mavis, after manning the Kabin for 24 years, moved to the Lake District to run a B&B. She gave her friend a picture of them together in the Kabin in the seventies as a memento. Rita's next sidekick was one-time sales rep Norris Cole – a fussing busybody – who like Mavis, often leaves a bemused Rita lost for words and raising her eyes heavenwards.

In 2004, Norris suspected that the Kabin was haunted after feeling an eerie breeze. When Emily told him the shop was built on the site of the old Mission where Ena Sharples' daughter, Vera Lomax, had died of a brain tumour in 1967, he organised a séance. He started proceedings by asking the ghost to 'knock once to signify your presence'. A box immediately fell off a shelf above his head. Blanche chortled, assuming Rita had planned it as a wind-up. But the group collectively shivered as Rita pulled her cardigan around her – she'd done no such thing. The next day, Charlie Stubbs, the builder, proposed a simpler solution – rising damp. While Norris was unconvinced, Rita rolled her eyes, vowing never to listen to his

LEFT: **He's the boss. Len counts the pennies in 1975**

BELOW: **Straight-talking Rita advises while Mavis dithers**

BELOW RIGHT: **Sharon finally realises Ian is a lying cheat in 1999**

THE KABIN

PROPRIETORS

1973–2009
RITA SULLIVAN

1999
SHARON GASKELL

2005–PRESENT
NORRIS COLE

2017
COLIN CALLEN

hare-brained schemes ever again.

Despite spending days side-by-side behind the counter, Rita and Norris also ended up on holiday together, when they won a trip to Hungary in 2006, leaving Ken Barlow manning the fort.

Norris, however, returned from the trip alone, explaining that Rita had broken her toes while they were away and had been forced to stay behind in hospital. But when a furious Rita later returned to Weatherfield, the truth came out – Norris had trodden on her foot in a desperate bid to beat her to the last bread roll on the buffet. In 2007, Norris got it into his head that he was going to propose to Rita – much to the relief of his landlady, Emily, who was worried he had set his sights on her. Over a candlelit meal, Rita let Norris down gently, explaining that he was a dear friend but she didn't want to marry him. Norris sulked for a few days before turning his attention to Rita's blousy showbiz pal, Doreen Fenwick, but to no avail.

Rita had always considered Norris to be a bit of an old woman, but it had never entered her head that he could be a cross-dresser. So when Emily displayed a thong and some lacy panties in the Kabin and announced that they belonged to Norris, he had some explaining to do. He said the lingerie was the prize in a competition, which he had won by writing about his dream date with Pierce Brosnan, using the entry name 'Noretta Cole'. And no, he added rather too loudly in the Rovers, he was not a transvestite.

Norris's hobby brought him into contact with rival competition addict Mary Taylor. By pooling their talents they won a motor home, but Norris's enthusiasm waned when the lonely Mary made it clear that he was the real prize. Threatened with seduction, he hastily made his excuses and left.

In September 2009, Norris used the money left to him by his half-brother Ramsay to buy out Rita. Ramsay's death had made Rita realise that it was time to take things easier. So while Rita set off on a long cruise, Norris became sole proprietor – not so much a newsagent as a veritable goliath of the retail trade.

When Rita returned from her cruise in early 2010, she wasn't ready to retire. So she worked at The Kabin again, but this time as Norris's newest employee. However, with grand dame Rita back behind the counter it soon became clear who was really in charge!

But The Kabin was almost the death of Rita, when she was trapped in the building during the tram crash in December 2010. Rita was reaching for a box on a high shelf when the shop was rocked by the explosion, and Rita was knocked to the ground. Luckily, Norris and Emily Bishop soon realised she was missing and raised the alarm.

Despite his reputation as a nosey gossip, Norris does look out for his friends. So when Rita's old flame Dennis Tanner returned to Weatherfield after 43 years away, Norris kept a close eye on the dodgy dealer. Rita and Dennis married in 2012, but Norris still disapproved of 'freeloader' Dennis who was mostly unemployed and had his head turned by Rita's Rovers Return rival, Gloria Price. But Dennis's 'free meal ticket' ran out when he punched Norris and gave him a bloody nose, and Rita entered The Kabin to catch Dennis

stealing from the till. She sent him packing as fast as the Wayfarer bus could carry him.

It was almost the end of an era in 2017, when Colin Callen, former owner of a chain of newsagents and wearer of loud shirts, persuaded Norris to sell The Kabin to him. Worse still, he manipulated Rita into selling the flat above while she was in hospital recovering from surgery for a brain tumour. Rita later regretted signing on the dotted line, but crafty Colin had no sympathy and refused to let Rita out of the deal. Fortunately, local legal eagle Adam Barlow found a way to blackmail Colin into selling back the flat and the Kabin to their rightful owners, Rita and Norris, meaning normal service was swiftly resumed behind the counter.

ABOVE: **Is there anybody there? Rita, Norris, Blanche and Betty hold a ghostly séance in 2004** ABOVE RIGHT: **Norris is attacked in the Kabin** RIGHT: **Rita is reunited with old flame Dennis Tanner and the pair get married in 2012** BOTTOM RIGHT: **Rita's in peril when she is trapped in the shop during the Weatherfield tram crash in 2010**

Song Of A Scarlet Summer
by Mavis Riley

As Rosalin's tender love song reache
it's climax, every word became a
personal message for Lionel who she
hoped desperately was sitting somewher
out there in the semi-darkness of the
night. Suddenly she heard a

The wives and times of Mr Baldwin

Factory boss Mike Baldwin might have been a cocky wheeler-dealer somewhat lacking in the empathetic touch – but there were still a few reasons to feel sorry for him.

Firstly, he was ripped off more times than the knickers he sold, thanks to the likes of Greg Kelly, Julia Stone and Joe Carter. His place of business had a habit of burning down on a regular basis, and he was forever losing everything he'd worked so hard for and having to start again. But above all of that, Mike deserved some sympathy for managing to hold his own in the factory for 30 years, despite being surrounded by some of the mouthiest, most intimidating women Coronation Street has ever known.

THE FACTORY

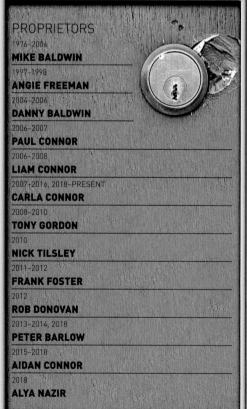

PROPRIETORS

1976–2006
MIKE BALDWIN

1997–1998
ANGIE FREEMAN

2004–2006
DANNY BALDWIN

2006–2007
PAUL CONNOR

2006–2008
LIAM CONNOR

2007–2016, 2018–PRESENT
CARLA CONNOR

2008–2010
TONY GORDON

2010
NICK TILSLEY

2011–2012
FRANK FOSTER

2012
ROB DONOVAN

2013–2014, 2018
PETER BARLOW

2015–2018
AIDAN CONNOR

2018
ALYA NAZIR

> Love me or loathe me, you've got to admit I've got style.
>
> **MIKE**

ABOVE: **Feisty machinists Ida Clough and Ivy Tilsley plan more industrial action in 1980**
BELOW: **Hilda snoops as Ivy sews**

Arriving in Weatherfield in 1976, having bought the Street's gutted warehouse, a weaker man would have cracked under the pressure of dealing with the staff Mike employed over the years. Among them, bolshie union rep Ivy Tilsley, her gobby mate Vera Duckworth, the formidable Elsie Tanner, sour-faced Ida Clough, acid-tongued Janice Battersby, outspoken Fiz Brown, attitude-laden Karen McDonald and sly Linda Sykes – the machinist who was to claw her way to the top, becoming the fourth Mrs Baldwin.

With an ever-present cigar in hand, Mike played up to his hard-as-nails image and rarely let his softer side come through. Although when he did, people were often surprised to find that the brash Baldwin's Casuals boss did have a heart after all.

For instance, when employee Ernest Bishop was killed by gunmen raiding the place for cash, Mike blamed himself and paid for the funeral. He offered widow Emily any financial help she needed and always looked out for her.

Ordinarily, however, Mike would rather stitch smalls himself than cough up any cash from his own pockets – often to his cost in the long run.

When Hilda Ogden needed a new broom to clean the factory with, Mike refused to stump up the cash because he was convinced she was going to use it at home as well. Insulted, Hilda let rip at her heartless boss, who sacked her. When Ivy called a union meeting to demand Hilda's reinstatement and Mike refused, the girls went out on strike, leading a stubborn Mike trying to man the sewing machines himself. Finally, following a riot outside, which saw the company van smashed up and a factory window broken, Mike gave Hilda her job back. All because of a miserable broom.

Hilda may well have been one of the few women in Weatherfield who escaped Mike's romantic intentions. A lifelong lothario, there were many ladies in his life. In fact, there was a point in the late seventies when he'd dated practically every female on the Street, while the early eighties saw him embark on a passionate affair with the newly married Deirdre Barlow.

Mike obviously had a thing about Barlows, as it was Susan Barlow who finally whisked the confirmed bachelor up the aisle in 1986. Susan was 23 years Mike's junior, and the relationship resulted in yet another left hook from Susan's father and Mike's arch-rival Ken when he found out they were together. But Mike was in love, and the fact that the girl in his bed was Ken's daughter made his joy even sweeter.

By now heading towards middle age, Mike wanted children as soon as possible, but Susan was determined to put her career first. When she eventually discovered she was pregnant, she shocked Mike by revealing she'd had a secret abortion. He accused her of killing their marriage and turned to drink when she left him. It was therefore a huge surprise in 2001 when Susan reappeared – along with Mike's son, Adam, who she had brought up in Glasgow unbeknown to the rest of the family. It turned out she had lied about the termination.

Romance blossomed again for Mike in 1989 when he fell for wide-eyed divorcee and cafe owner, Alma Sedgewick. But with his business in serious trouble, Mike put money before love and wormed his way into the affections of Jackie Ingram, his new business partner, who was also a very rich woman thanks to the fact that her husband – one of Mike's competitors – had recently dropped dead. Their marriage ended after two weeks, when it finally clicked for Jackie that her new husband was more interested in her bank balance than her. Feeling bitterly betrayed, Jackie threatened a terrified Mike with a loaded shotgun before leaving him.

In 1992, Mike finally apologised to Alma – who was now going out with Ken Barlow – and begged her to marry him. They spent several happy years together, and it looked like Mike Baldwin had finally settled down.

However, in 1999 it all went pear-shaped when, in a moment of weakness, Mike cheated on Alma with con artist Julia Stone, who then blackmailed him. When Alma found out, she was devastated. She left him and moved into Audrey's.

During their separation, Mike's most rough and ready Underworld machinist, Linda Sykes, decided to make her move and seduced her boss – even

> ‘Mike Baldwin is a vampire, draining the life out of people, destroying lives...’

KEN BARLOW

93

ABOVE LEFT: **The legendary ladies' man finally settles down with Susan Barlow in 1986** ABOVE: **When Alma met Jackie in 1991** BELOW LEFT: **Mess with the women of Baldwin's Casuals at your peril, 1989** BELOW RIGHT: **The factory girls prepare for the McDonald wedding of the year**

RIGHT: **Audrey reads this poem by Mary Elizabeth Frye at Alma Baldwin's funeral in 2001. At the wake, Alma appears in a video message saying a final goodbye to her friends and family.**

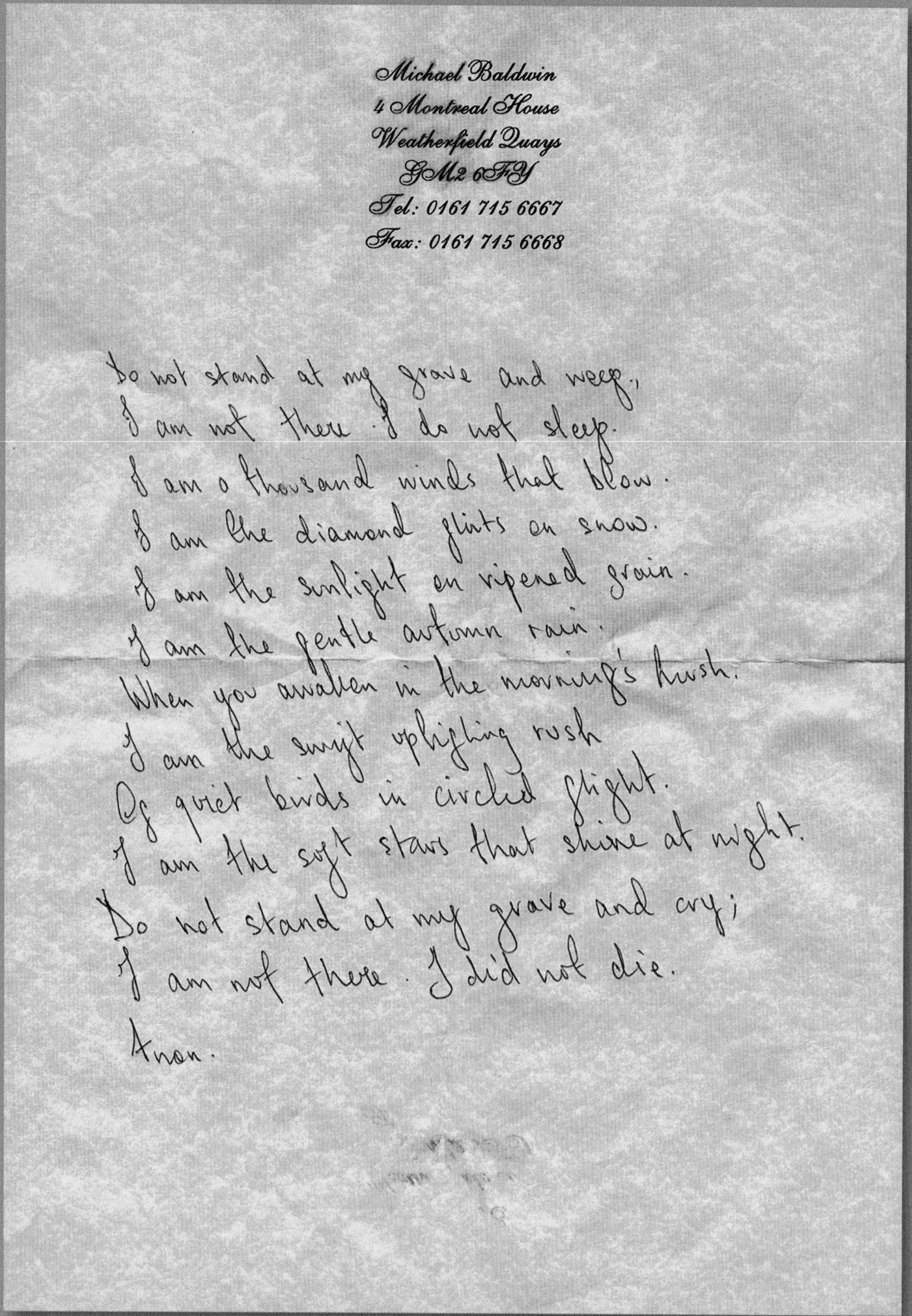

Michael Baldwin
4 Montreal House
Weatherfield Quays
GM2 6FY
Tel: 0161 715 6667
Fax: 0161 715 6668

Do not stand at my grave and weep,
I am not there. I do not sleep.
I am a thousand winds that blow.
I am the diamond glints on snow.
I am the sunlight on ripened grain.
I am the gentle autumn rain.
When you awaken in the morning's hush.
I am the swift uplifting rush
Of quiet birds in circled flight.
I am the soft stars that shine at night.
Do not stand at my grave and cry;
I am not there. I did not die.

Anon.

RIGHT: **Clocking on! Janice worked as a factory machinist for over a decade. Remember when she almost burned the place down by dropping her cigarette?**

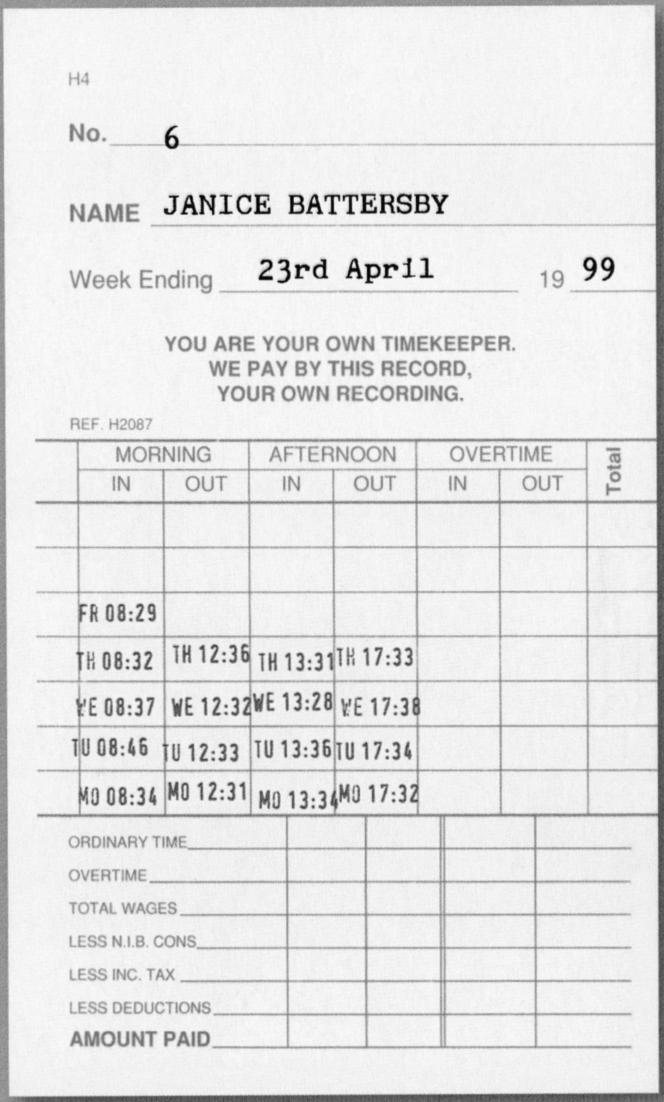

H4

No. **6**

NAME **JANICE BATTERSBY**

Week Ending **23rd April** 19 **99**

YOU ARE YOUR OWN TIMEKEEPER.
WE PAY BY THIS RECORD,
YOUR OWN RECORDING.

REF. H2087

	MORNING		AFTERNOON		OVERTIME		Total
	IN	OUT	IN	OUT	IN	OUT	
FR 08:29							
TH 08:32	TH 12:36	TH 13:31	TH 17:33				
WE 08:37	WE 12:32	WE 13:28	WE 17:38				
TU 08:46	TU 12:33	TU 13:36	TU 17:34				
MO 08:34	MO 12:31	MO 13:34	MO 17:32				

ORDINARY TIME

OVERTIME

TOTAL WAGES

LESS N.I.B. CONS

LESS INC. TAX

LESS DEDUCTIONS

AMOUNT PAID

though he was old enough to be her father. Linda soon moved into Mike's quayside flat and enjoyed the trappings of his wealth almost as much as dumping all of Alma's belongings into bin bags.

Humiliated, Alma divorced Mike, clearing the way for Linda to marry him in September 2000. But Linda had secretly been having a lusty affair with Mike's son – and his best man – Mark Redman for months. At the reception, a drunken Mark was unable to cope with the guilt any longer and, to Linda's horror, he confessed all to his father. Thinking quickly, Linda insisted Mark had forced her into the fling and Mike, still beguiled by his cunning bride, believed her. He chose a future with Linda and banished his distraught son.

But the honeymoon with Linda was soon over when Mike found out from Audrey Roberts that Alma was dying from cancer. It hit him harder than he could ever have expected and, much to Linda's dismay, he rushed to Alma at the Lake District hotel where she was resting. Mike opened up to Alma as he never had before – admitting he had been a fool to let her go. It took the realisation that he was soon to lose the best thing that ever happened to him, to make Mike Baldwin show his true emotions at last.

Back at Audrey's, Mike kept a round-the-clock vigil at Alma's bedside during her last few days. He played her favourite Perry Como tape to her as she drifted in and out of consciousness, and when Linda suggested she could stay and help Mike in a belated attempt to get back into his good books, he told her to get lost. Alma died peacefully in her bed and tears of loss and regret poured down Mike's face.

In 2004, Mike decided to take more of a back seat at Underworld and invited his nephew, Danny, to join him in the business. A year on, a skeleton came tumbling out of the cupboard when it was revealed that Danny was not Mike's nephew – he was in fact his son, the result of a fling with his sister-in-law, Viv.

Later that year, Mike was diagnosed with Alzheimer's disease, and soon he began to get confused over dates and who people were. When Deirdre visited him at his flat, she was shocked to discover Mike thought they were still a couple.

Not wanting to upset her old friend and lover, Deirdre agreed when he asked her to dance, sobbing silently over his shoulder as they swayed around the living room. It was hard for his friends to watch a once-powerful man like Mike being beaten by such a debilitating disease. But for Danny – egged on by his girlfriend Leanne Battersby – it was an opportunity to get his hands on Mike's estate and to leave his rival for the empire, half-brother Adam, with nothing.

After contracting pneumonia, Mike died of a heart attack, ironically in the arms of his lifelong nemesis Ken Barlow. His last words were typical Baldwin fighting talk. He gasped, 'You're finished, Barlow. Deirdre loves me, she's mine.'

Yet the Baldwins' family dramas were positively tame compared to those of the next owners of Underworld, the Connors. Cheating boss Paul Connor was killed in a car accident after discovering the prostitute he had ordered was Leanne Battersby, his brother Liam's latest girlfriend. Liam's response was to bed Paul's glamorous, hard-nosed widow Carla, even though by then he had just married Maria Sutherland, and Carla was engaged to businessman Tony Gordon. When Tony found out, he cunningly asked Liam to be his best man and then arranged for him to be killed in a hit-and-run on the stag night. Although struggling to come to terms with Liam's death, Carla went ahead and married Tony.

Shown mobile phone footage of Carla and Liam kissing, Maria deduced that Tony was somehow responsible for her husband's death and daubed the word 'Murderer' outside the factory. The only person to believe her was pensioner Jed Stone, who had previously witnessed Tony's evil side when the latter had tried to evict him from his home. Now blackmailed by Jed, Tony strangled him in a fit of rage just before the 2008 Underworld Christmas party. He hid the body at the factory, but when he returned on

> ## You might not be a priest, Roy Cropper, but you're the best I have.
>
> **TONY GORDON CONFESSING TO LIAM'S MURDER**

ABOVE LEFT: **Machinist Linda Sykes gets her claws into Mike, 1999** ABOVE RIGHT: **Mark finally comes clean to his newlywed dad in 2000** BELOW LEFT: **Kelly does her best to turn Sean** BOTTOM RIGHT: **Nick rescues Janice from the factory fire in 2004**

Christmas Day, Jed was still alive. Tony bought Jed's silence by offering him a free flat in Wigan, where he was visited by a suspicious Carla. Noticing the red marks on Jed's neck, she realised that Tony had tried to strangle him. Tony confessed to his role in Liam's murder and, in fear for her own safety, she fled Weatherfield. Tony attempted to assuage his guilt by supporting Maria through her pregnancy, but when Carla returned in 2009, the shock caused him to suffer a near-fatal heart attack. After almost killing Roy Cropper, he finally admitted everything to the police, seemingly bringing to an end a chapter in Underworld's turbulent history.

But in a dramatic turn of events, Tony escaped from prison a few months later. He hotfooted it back to Coronation Street and held Carla hostage at Underworld, before setting it ablaze. However, Carla is made of tough stuff, and you cross her at your own peril. After shooting Tony she escaped his clutches, and her deranged hubby was killed when the factory exploded in flames moments later.

After her nightmare at the hands of Tony, Carla should have learned a lesson about mixing business and pleasure. Unfortunately, she fell for Frank Foster a year later. Frank bought shares in the factory and he and Carla got engaged. But the night before their wedding, Frank raped Carla when he discovered she was in love with Peter Barlow. Frank was charged with the crime but hired a private investigator to discredit Carla and

Peter's evidence against him and he walked free. Justice was ultimately served, Weatherfield-style, when Frank was later found murdered in the factory. Carla and Peter topped a long list of suspects but the real culprit turned out to be Frank's mother, Anne, sickened to overhear him gloating about the rape.

After owning the factory for over a decade, the Connors almost lost it in 2017, when a vengeful Adam Barlow, from whom the clan had bought their original share of the business, joined forces with Aidan Connor's bitter fiancée Eva Price to put the factory out of action. Eva, who hated Aidan for cheating on her with best friend Maria, later regretted her actions, but Adam was confidently smug when Underworld was stripped of all its assets, including the roof.

But when the Connor family are knocked down, they get back up. Aidan and Carla, helped by former trainee manager Alya Nazir, got the place running again. But less than a month after becoming sole owner of the business, depressed Aidan took his own life in May 2018. When Aidan's will was read, the Connors were dismayed to learn he had left the factory to Alya.

As a bitter power struggle for control of the factory began, Carla dug in her designer heels and emerged triumphant, making it very clear to Alya and the rest of Weatherfield: the Connors will never surrender their business empire without an almighty fight!

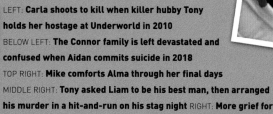

LEFT: **Carla shoots to kill when killer hubby Tony holds her hostage at Underworld in 2010**
BELOW LEFT: **The Connor family is left devastated and confused when Aidan commits suicide in 2018**
TOP RIGHT: **Mike comforts Alma through her final days**
MIDDLE RIGHT: **Tony asked Liam to be his best man, then arranged his murder in a hit-and-run on his stag night** RIGHT: **More grief for the Connors as Paul perishes in 2007** BELOW RIGHT: **Sally is a suspect when hated factory boss Frank is found murdered in 2012**

Marriage made in a greasy spoon

It was the happiest moment of their lives, as Roy Cropper and Hayley Patterson tied the knot at Roy's Rolls on their chaotic wedding day in April 1999. But the couple were celebrating more than just their marriage – they were celebrating their acceptance. Outsiders Roy and Hayley were now fully fledged members of the community and as near to married as they could possibly be, considering Hayley's transsexual status.

The wedding preparations had been anything but smooth – mealy-mouthed Blanche Hunt disapproved and nasty-minded Linda Sykes refused to attend, saying, 'If I want to go to the circus, I'll book the Big Top.' Meanwhile, money-grabbing Les Battersby had sold the story to the tabloids, resulting in the bride and groom being hounded out of the church before the service had even begun. As wedding guest Emily Bishop wisely put it, 'The sad truth is, I'm afraid, that Mr Battersby is not alone in disliking what he doesn't understand.'

Back at Roy's Rolls, it looked like the whole thing was off, with Hayley in tears upstairs in the flat being comforted by Alma. But Roy had a brainwave and, in the end, they married in the cafe with a touching, dignified ceremony surrounded by their moist-eyed friends and neighbours. Hayley revealed she had already changed her name by deed poll to Cropper, and with that the pair left for a romantic honeymoon touring the railway museums of York.

The besotted couple had come a long way. When Roy first appeared in Weatherfield, he was the anorak-wearing recluse neighbour of Deirdre at the grotty Crimea Street flats, and no-one knew what to make of him. Hayley, meanwhile, had her own issues, and whilst working at Firman's Freezers, was introduced to Roy by mutual friend Alma. Almost immediately, they realised they were kindred spirits.

In 1997, Roy used his life savings to buy Alma's share of Jim's Cafe for £35,000, eventually changing the name to Roy's Rolls. In 1999, he decided to move to new premises on Victoria Street and has been dishing out barm cakes and greasy chips ever since.

Roy and Hayley longed for children and, after becoming godparents to Bethany Platt in 2000, they decided that fostering would be their best option: they looked after a young boy, Wayne, who they found stealing food in the cafe; a well-behaved girl called Jackie; and troublesome but misunderstood teen Fiz Brown, who was later to become one of their most ardent friends.

Roy and Hayley's biggest chance of a child they could call their own came in 2003, when Tracy Barlow drugged Roy and pretended she had slept with him for a bet. A few weeks later Tracy was pregnant, insisting he was the father. The Croppers decided to adopt the baby and paid Tracy in cash. Meanwhile, Roy demanded that she marry him, in name only, to make sure he had a legal right to the child. The couple adored baby Patience – later renamed Amy – and when Tracy took her away from them, finally owning up to the fact that Steve McDonald was the father, they were heartbroken.

So Hayley was in for a hell of a shock in 2007 when she discovered that, in her former life as 'Harold', she had unwittingly fathered a son.

The bombshell came when she attended the funeral of her Aunt Monica and found a letter

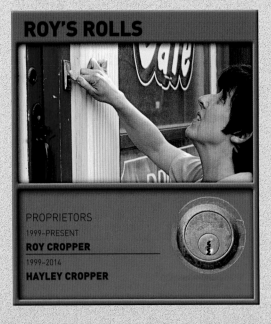

ROY'S ROLLS

PROPRIETORS
1999–PRESENT
ROY CROPPER

1999–2014
HAYLEY CROPPER

TOP: **Alma agrees to sell her share of the cafe to Roy in 1997**
ABOVE: **A marriage of acceptance. Roy and Hayley finally tie the knot in 1999**
RIGHT: **Roy's not the daddy. Giving up baby Patience in 2004**

ASSORTED PIES

addressed to Harold while sorting through a box of her aunt's things. It was from a boy called Christian who was trying to track down his dad. Hayley was initially so shocked by this reminder of her deeply unhappy past that her first reaction was to immediately rip the letter to shreds. But deep down, the machinist knew she had to find her son – the child she'd always dreamt of having. Hayley was worried about how Roy would react to the news. After all, she'd told him she was a virgin when they'd married. Desperate for someone to talk to, she confided in gobby café employee and scarily over-protective friend Becky Granger, who suggested getting a private detective on the case. When Hayley did eventually tell a bewildered Roy about her son, the café owner insisted she must tell Christian the truth about her past.

When Hayley met Christian, however, she bottled it and introduced herself as his long-lost aunt, telling her inquisitive son that Harold was dead. Eventually, Hayley resigned herself to being honest with Christian, but he reacted badly to Hayley's admission that she used to be Harold, lashing out at her and leaving her sobbing and bruised on the ground. This was a development which didn't go down too well with no-nonsense Becky. She promptly stomped round to Christian's shop and belted him for the way he'd treated Hayley.

After a sorely needed, three-week camping trip to recover from their recent emotional turmoil, Hayley became set on the idea of travelling to Africa with Roy to help underprivileged children. When only one place became available on the trip, however, Roy persuaded Hayley to follow her dream, saying that if anyone deserved the chance to do some good in the world, it was her.

Despite hiding his discontent behind his duty to serve all-day breakfasts, Roy was soon pining for Hayley and decided to visit her in Africa, leaving the café in the capable hands of Becky and Ken Barlow. On his return, he gave a job to Anna Windass, whose layabout partner Eddie secretly used Roy's account card for shopping trips to the cash and carry. The store proclaimed Eddie (masquerading as Roy) to be its millionth customer and the winner of a free holiday – a fact it advertised by placing life-sized cardboard cut-outs around the premises. Sadly for Eddie, although the cut-outs were of his face and body, they bore the name 'Roy Cropper', and when Hayley spotted them, the game was up.

It was Roy's misfortune to discover Tony Gordon lying in the street after his heart attack. Convinced that he was about to die, Tony confessed his sins to Roy, but when he unexpectedly recovered, he resolved to silence Roy by drowning him in the canal. As Roy floundered helplessly in the water, Tony had a sudden change of heart and dived in to rescue him. Roy had lived to butter baps for another day.

In 2011, customers at the greasy spoon suddenly found their full English breakfast and cup of tea served with an unwanted helping of snooty rudeness when Roy's outspoken mum, Sylvia Goodwin, arrived in Weatherfield and began helping behind the counter.

The formidable pensioner considered the café 'a sinking ship' and decided to get 'the till ringing' by introducing controversial new rules, including making customers pay extra for condiments, chucking out anyone who overstayed their welcome and charging for use of the 'water closet'. When Norris Cole refused to pay the 20 pence fee and sneakily tried to use the toilet for free, Sylvia locked the penny-pinching newsagent in the WC overnight.

But Roy has always been a stickler for tradition. So it was a step too far when American businessman Milton Fanshaw, who romanced Sylvia on a Caribbean cruise, suggested turning Roy's Rolls into an American style diner. No thank-you. Roy liked the café menu just the way it was.

Tragedy struck when Hayley was diagnosed with terminal pancreatic cancer in 2013. Rather than suffer a long, painful demise, Hayley chose to end her own life at home with Roy by her side at the start of the New Year.

Roy lost his way for a while after losing Hayley and certainly wasn't looking for love again. But he gradually began to grow close to widow Cathy Matthews, who he met at the garden allotments, and the pair almost made it down the aisle in December 2016. But realising Roy was still in love with Hayley and marrying her out of obligation, Cathy jilted Roy and the pair decided they were better off as friends.

99

ABOVE LEFT: **Toilet trouble. Snooty Sylvia teaches naughty Norris a lesson** ABOVE RIGHT: **Roy has a lucky escape** ABOVE RIGHT: **Eddie Windass is found out** RIGHT: **Roy and Hayley get married (again!) in 2010** BELOW: **Roy's beloved wife Hayley is diagnosed with pancreatic cancer** BELOW, RIGHT: **Roy begins a romance with widow Cathy in 2015**

RIGHT: **A series of Roy Cropper's (very straight-faced) passport photos.**

A.

This Change of Name Deed (intended to be enrolled at

the Central Office) made this *16th* day of *April 1999*

By me the undersigned

of *16 Victoria street. Weatherfield. Greater Manchester.*

(¹)

now or lately called *Hayley Anne Cropper.*

a (²)[British citizen/~~British Dependent Territories citizen/British Overseas citizen~~]

(²)[Commonwealth citizen]

under section(³) *37 (1)* of the British Nationality Act 1981.

Witnesses and it is hereby declared (⁴)[~~on behalf of myself my wife and my children~~] as follows: —

(1) Describe as "single", "married", "widowed" or "divorced".

(2) Make the appropriate deletions so as to describe the applicant correctly in accordance with para. 2 of S.I. 1994 No. 604.

(3) Insert the number of the relevant section. In the case of an applicant described as a "Commonwealth citizen" the relevant section is 37(1).

(4) Delete such of the words in brackets as are inapplicable.

1. I absolutely and entirely renounce relinquish and abandon the use of my said former surname of

and assume adopt and determine to take and use from the date hereof the surname of *Cropper* in substitution for my former surname of *Patterson*

2. I shall at all times hereafter in all records deeds documents and other writings and in all actions and proceedings as well as in all dealings and transactions and on all occasions whatsoever use and subscribe the said name of *Cropper* as my surname in substitution for my former surname of *Patterson* so relinquished as aforesaid to the intent that I (⁴)[~~my wife and my children~~] may hereafter be called known or distinguished not by the former surname of *Patterson* but by the surname of *Cropper* only.

3. I authorise and require all persons at all times to designate describe and address me (⁴)[my wife and my children] by the adopted surname of *Cropper*

In Witness whereof I have hereunto subscribed my first name or names of *Hayley Anne* and my adopted and substituted surname of *Cropper* and also my said former surname of *Patterson* the day and year first above written.

This is the Deed marked A referred to in the Declaration of and produced and shown

A Commissioner for Oaths

on making the said Declaration before me this

to h

day of

(5) The Official regulations for enrolment require the Deed to be signed in both the old and new names.

(6) Two Witnesses.

Signed as a Deed and delivered by the above-named

in the presence of(⁶)

Hayley Cropper

(⁵)[formerly known as

Hayley Patterson   ]

101

No place like gnome for the Wiltons

Many a man has been smitten with Mavis Riley, but unfortunately she always seemed to attract the drippier of the male species. For years, she was torn between insipid poetry-loving artist type Victor Pendlebury and weedy sales rep Derek Wilton – but after various failed engagements and churchyard jiltings, it was Derek whom she finally married in 1988.

If ever there was a person who was the butt of more jokes than anyone else, it had to be hapless but harmless Derek. The one-time Envirosphere humidifier salesman had no sense of humour and with his Mile Muncher running machine, garden gnomes Arthur and Guinevere, and giant-paperclipped car, he was an easy target. For next-door neighbour Des Barnes, winding up Derek was a daily pastime.

It was during the summer of 1995 that Derek noticed one of his treasured gnomes, Arthur, had gone from his garden. He received a postcard from Arthur – in Eastbourne! Soon postcards started arriving from around the world. Incensed, Mavis and Derek were convinced Des was the culprit and confronted him. But the bookie swore blind he had better things to do with his time than send postcards from a gnome.

Things came to a head when a hand-delivered parcel arrived at No.4. Inside, Derek discovered a shoebox containing a severed gnome's ear and a ransom note instructing him to leave 50 chocolate doubloons by the swings on the Red Rec, otherwise next time he'd be receiving more than just Arthur's ear in the post. Mavis pleaded with Derek not to go, but he was a man on a mission and headed for the park. Whilst waiting for the handover, he lurked in the bushes when, to his horror, he was arrested on suspicion of being the local flasher.

It was only when Derek was staying at Norris Cole's on the eve of Norris's wedding that he discovered Arthur hidden in a wardrobe. Norris confessed all, and the next day as revenge – in an unusual moment of cunning – best man Derek took Norris to the wrong church, making him late for his own wedding.

In 1997, Derek had a heart attack in his car during a road-rage incident. At the funeral, a devastated Mavis turned on the mourners, saying, 'You thought us figures of fun. Well, it doesn't matter to me, because I loved him, and I know he loved me.'

The end terrace also held difficult memories for caring butcher Ashley Peacock, who moved into the house, owned by his father Fred Elliott, in 1997. The front room is where, six years later, Richard Hillman brutally murdered Ashley's young wife, Maxine, with a crowbar. His intended victim had been elderly investor and babysitter Emily Bishop. But when Maxine came home early from a party to check on little Joshua, her fate was sealed, leaving Ashley a broken-hearted widower.

Those were dark days for Ashley. But eventually he realised he needed help at home. He hired a sweet-natured nanny, Claire Casey, and the pair fell in love. An emotional Christmas Day ceremony in 2004 meant Ashley, finally put the past behind him and build a new life with Claire and Joshua.

The death of his foghorn-voiced father, Fred Elliott, in 2006 proved to be a trying time for

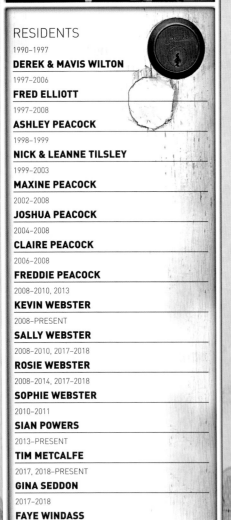

NO **4 CORONATION ST.**

RESIDENTS

1990–1997
DEREK & MAVIS WILTON

1997–2006
FRED ELLIOTT

1997–2008
ASHLEY PEACOCK

1998–1999
NICK & LEANNE TILSLEY

1999–2003
MAXINE PEACOCK

2002–2008
JOSHUA PEACOCK

2004–2008
CLAIRE PEACOCK

2006–2008
FREDDIE PEACOCK

2008–2010, 2013
KEVIN WEBSTER

2008–PRESENT
SALLY WEBSTER

2008–2010, 2017–2018
ROSIE WEBSTER

2008–2014, 2017–2018
SOPHIE WEBSTER

2010–2011
SIAN POWERS

2013–PRESENT
TIM METCALFE

2017, 2018–PRESENT
GINA SEDDON

2017–2018
FAYE WINDASS

TOP RIGHT: **Mavis and the rivals for her attention – Derek and Victor Pendlebury**
MIDDLE RIGHT: **Derek confronts Norris about his disappearing gnome, 1995**
BELOW RIGHT: **Grub's up at the Wiltons'**

Ashley. Fred died on the morning of his wedding day at Audrey Roberts' house, wrongly convincing his fiancée, Bev Unwin, that he had been having an affair.

In 2007, tragedy struck at No.4 when the house became engulfed by flames. With Ashley and Joshua away, Jamie Baldwin and Kirk Sutherland managed to rescue Claire, but the Peacocks' new son Freddie was nowhere to be found. The police then revealed that the fire had been started deliberately. Due to her previous battles with postnatal depression, Claire was arrested but then released and Freddie was discovered unharmed in a local park. The real culprit was Claire's mentally unstable former friend Casey, who had wanted Claire's life for herself. Feeling unsupported by her husband, Claire moved out and Casey seized her moment to make a move, taking advantage of vulnerable Ashley and seducing him. Eventually, a deranged Casey was arrested for snatching Freddie, and Claire and Ashley's nightmare was finally over.

Sally was constantly badgering Kevin to move from No.13. She had always fancied somewhere bigger – just like the Peacocks' house. So when Claire revealed that she and Ashley were considering downsizing because of their money troubles, Sally suggested that the families swap houses. She even managed to persuade Kevin, who was usually harder to shift than dry rot. Thus in July 2008, after the women had haggled endlessly over the price, the Peacocks became the new residents of No 13.

The move did little to improve the Peacocks' fortunes. Claire collapsed at home, and when she was rushed to hospital, she learned that she had been pregnant but had suffered a miscarriage. Afraid of a recurrence of her postnatal depression, she decided she didn't want any more children and ordered Ashley to get a vasectomy. Ashley reluctantly agreed but couldn't go through with it, causing a frosty Claire to slap a sex ban on him.

RIGHT: **Ashley discovers Maxine murdered in the front room in 2003** FAR RIGHT: **Claire and Ashley marry on Christmas Day, 2004** BELOW RIGHT: **Fred drops dead on his wedding day**

The frustration proved unbearable, however, and finally he made another appointment to have the operation. He was one Peacock who wouldn't be quite so proud for a while.

Despite the house swap, the curse of No.13 followed the Websters to No.4. Kevin began an affair with his workmate Tyrone Dobbs' wife, Molly. On Christmas Day 2009, Kevin was about to tell his wife he was leaving her for Molly, when a tearful Sally dropped the bombshell she'd been diagnosed with breast cancer. It was almost a year before Sally discovered his betrayal, and that he was also the father of Molly's baby son Jack.

Despite their bitter break-up, Sally and Kevin eventually found a way to move on as friends for the sake of their daughters, Rosie and Sophie. Sally eventually found love again with window cleaner Tim Metcalfe, and to everyone's relief, he and Kevin became great buddies. When Sally agreed to marry Tim in 2015, Tim asked Kevin to be his best man.

Tim has gotten used to Sally's snooty high standards over time, which have involved an over-the-garden-fence squabble with next-door-neighbour Anna Windass over a bottle of ketchup, and the time Sally shut down Tim's infamous home brewery, which exploded all over her beloved conservatory. But while they squabble, just like other couples on the Street, it never takes long for Sally and Tim to kiss and make up over a drink in the Rovers or a nice tea at home.

Luckily, Sally found the perfect platform for her moral crusades when she was elected Mayor of Weatherfield in Autumn 2017. She won by 51 votes over rival Kirk Sutherland, who, much to the annoyance of Kirk's partner Beth, helped Sally by handing out some of her campaign flyers. Whether it involved quoting French feminist writer Simone de Beauvoir when reprimanding sexist builders, or dealing with every day issues like litter and parking, Sally set out to make a 'small but vital difference in people's lives'.

Unfortunately, Sally's determination to help one man in particular proved to be her undoing, when she chose Duncan Radfield as the recipient of a substantial charity grant of £40,000. Duncan did a flit with the cash, leaving Sally facing some tough questions from the council and even tougher ones from the police. Forced to resign as mayor and return to her job at Underworld full-time, Sally vowed Duncan would be the last smooth-talking charmer to pull the wool over her eyes.

BELOW LEFT: **Sophie falls in love with her best friend Sian** BELOW MIDDLE: **Stubborn Sally still expects to marry Tim even though the groom has told her the wedding is off** BELOW: **Food fight! Neighbours Sally and Anna squabble over the tomato sauce**

RIGHT: **Who has kidnapped Derek Wilton's beloved garden gnome Arthur and sent him this ransom note? The culprit is later unmasked and revealed to be Derek's friend Norris Cole!**

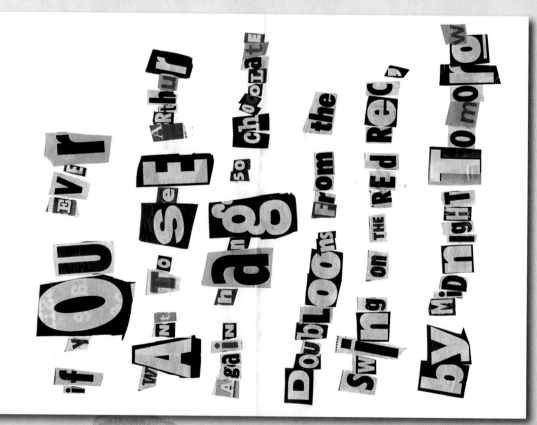

RIGHT: **Jealous of all the attention older sister Rosie is getting, troublesome teenager Sophie sends a postcard to her parents pretending her life is in danger.**

HAVE A NICE DAY! ☺

Sophie's nEXT

© Have a Nice Day ltd. 2008

MR And mrS K webSTer
4 coronAtion streEt
weAtherfiELD
mmo Tig

105

HAVE A NICE DAY!

Tragedy behind closed doors

№ 6 CORONATION ST.

RESIDENTS

1990–1991
STEPH BARNES

1990–1998
DES BARNES

1998–1999
NATALIE BARNES

2000
DEBS BROWNLOW

2000–2002
MATT & CHARLIE RAMSDEN

2002–2005
TOMMY, ANGELA, KATY & CRAIG HARRIS

2006–2007
CHARLIE STUBBS & TRACY BARLOW

2007–2008
JERRY, DARRYL, JODIE, MEL & KAYLEIGH MORTON

2008
TERESA BRYANT

2008–2014
ANNA & GARY WINDASS

2008–2011
EDDIE WINDASS

2011–2014
FAYE WINDASS

2012–2014
OWEN ARMSTRONG

2014–PRESENT
YASMEEN NAZIR

2014–2016
SHARIF NAZIR

2014–2015
KAL NAZIR

2014–2016, 2018–PRESENT
ALYA NAZIR

2014–2018
ZEEDAN NAZIR

2016–2018
RANA NAZIR

2016–2018
CATHY MATTHEWS

2017
AIDAN CONNOR

RIGHT: **Cleaner Phyllis Pearce took a shine to Des but rubbed flouncy Steph up the wrong way** BELOW: **They'd only been married a month. Natalie cradles her dying husband in 1998**

Bookie Des Barnes and his flouncy wife Steph moved into No.6 on their wedding day – the house was a gift from her father who had built the new Coronation Street development. Within days, Steph – who worked on the perfume counter at a department store – had made quite an impact on the Street and had even managed to lure a hopeful Kevin Webster upstairs, only to shave off his moustache. Theirs was a sparky relationship, yet Steph soon became bored with Des and life on Coronation Street, and left him a year later, in 1991, for an architect.

With Steph out of the picture, Des enjoyed the single life – playing rival barmaids Raquel Wolstenhulme and Tanya Pooley off against each other but ending up with neither. In 1998, he fell in love with and married another feisty Rovers barmaid, Natalie Horrocks. The champagne flowed at their wedding, but the return of Natalie's wayward son Tony to Weatherfield was to end their happiness.

One night at No.6, Tony was accosted by thugs who were looking for the drugs money that he owed them. Des happened on the scene as they were beating up Tony, and whilst trying to help his stepson, he took a blow to the head which sent him crashing into the coffee table. He died in hospital in Natalie's arms – they'd been married less than a month.

Childhood sweethearts Tommy and Angela Harris and their children Katy and Craig arrived at No.6 from Sheffield, but originally used the surname 'Nelson'. It turned out they'd been forced to join the witness-protection programme because Angela had received death threats after witnessing a murder and giving evidence in court.

However, in April 2003, strong-willed teenager Katy sneaked off to see her mates in Sheffield and was followed back to Weatherfield by other members of the gang Angela had helped convict. Tommy was shot by one of them but survived. With their cover blown, the family decided to make the Street their permanent home and hoped to put the upheavals of the past behind them.

But life became more complicated than they could ever have predicted. When schoolgirl Katy got together with nurse Martin Platt – who was old enough to be her father – hot-tempered Tommy

> **They spend more time falling out than breathing.**
>
> **AUDREY ROBERTS ON DES AND STEPH**

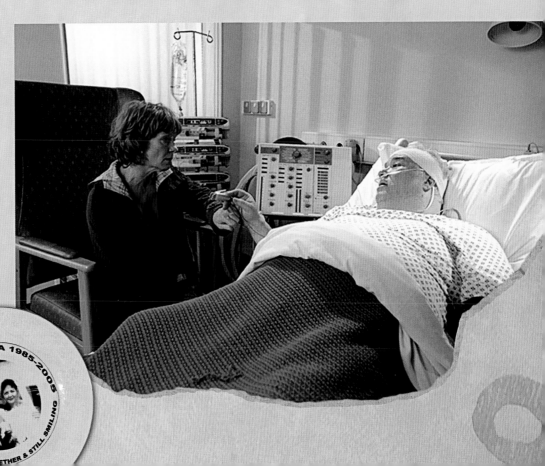

flipped. Craig blamed Martin for his parents' break-up and, by tampering with the brakes on a car, nearly killed both Martin and Katy. Tommy and Martin became firm enemies, but it was Katy's pregnancy that was to signal the tragic demise of the Harris family.

In March 2005, believing Martin was having an affair – a lie started by Tommy – a confused Katy had an abortion. However, she soon discovered the truth and realised, thanks to Tommy, she had now destroyed her relationship with Martin as well as their baby. Alone at the garage, Tommy gloated over what he'd done and Katy – still in emotional turmoil – snapped and lashed out at her dad with a wrench, killing him instantly.

Grief-stricken Angela managed to keep a straight head and when Tommy's body was found, both mother and daughter blamed it on Martin and the Sheffield crooks from their past. Eventually, Angela confessed, to spare Katy. Meanwhile, Craig, still unaware of the whole truth, struggled to cope without his dad.

But the guilt was too much for diabetic Katy. Alone at No.6, she smashed her insulin cartridges and then composed herself enough to write a confession letter. She then began spooning sugar into her mouth and was only saved by Martin, Sarah and Scooter as she began to black out. She died in hospital with a bereft Martin at her bedside.

There was more doom and gloom in store for No.6 when Weatherfield's all-time most volatile couple moved in – control freak Charlie Stubbs and über-bitch Tracy Barlow. Neither of them was averse to playing mind games, lying or using people, so when this pair got together, it seemed as though they had both finally met their match.

Ken and Deirdre disapproved of their daughter's latest beau, of course, but Tracy didn't care. Theirs was a passionate relationship, and she reckoned she could twist Charlie around her little finger – or so she thought. Like the time when she faked an abortion only to spend Charlie's termination cash on a new pair of shoes. When he

> ❝ I love you, Martin. And I want to spend the rest of my life with you and have your children, loads of children... ❞
>
> KATY

ABOVE LEFT: **Tommy and Angela aren't exactly chuffed about Martin and their teenage daughter Katy**

ABOVE: **A tragic end. Katy passes away in hospital in the company of Craig, Martin and her grandad, 2005**

BELOW: **Jerry Morton was left in the hands of his evil ex-wife, Teresa Bryant**

107

TOMMY & ANGELA 1985-2005
20 YEARS TOGETHER & STILL SMILING

found out, he infuriated her by ditching one of them in his skip. But this love-hate relationship was to end in murder when Tracy discovered Charlie had a one-night stand with his ex, Shelley, leaving Shelley pregnant. This was followed by a long-running affair with pretty hairdresser Maria, all behind Tracy's back. Apoplectic with rage, soon the only thing on Tracy's mind was punishing Charlie with the ultimate revenge. She started by convincing her neighbours that Charlie was abusing her, even burning herself with an iron in order to appear the battered victim. Later that month, Tracy went in for the kill. After lap dancing for Charlie and pretending she wanted to spend the rest of her life with him, she whacked him twice over the head with a weighty ornament before putting a knife into her lifeless boyfriend's hand. As Ken, Deirdre and Peter banged on the door, Tracy composed herself before sobbing to her family that she had acted in self-defence. However, much to Tracy's horror, Charlie was still alive. When he died in hospital three days later, she grinned evilly to herself like the cat that had got the cream.

But Tracy wasn't smiling when she was convicted of murder and sentenced to life imprisonment, having already told a bewildered Deirdre the horrible truth and begged her poor mother to lie for her in court. As Tracy was dragged screaming to the cells in front of her family and neighbours, she howled that she was innocent, but there was no going back. It seemed the lying and manipulative Tracy Barlow had cried wolf once too often.

Kebab shop owner Jerry Morton and his clan didn't linger long at No.6, and after Jerry suffered a heart attack while chasing a gang of tearaways, he decamped to Spain. But his manipulative ex-wife, Teresa Bryant, continued to hang around like a bad smell. Forever in search of a roof over her head, she had tried to keep Jerry in poor health by doctoring his medication so that he would need her around. When the Mortons left, she decided to barricade herself into the house. Unfortunately for her, the new residents – the Windasses – were not renowned for observing

social niceties and wasted no time in throwing her out onto the street.

If Anna Windass represented the respectable face of the family, Eddie was the polar opposite. With his unkempt mane and a fake limp that switched from one leg to the other depending on which Social Security officer was spying on him, he was a scrounger of the first order, his only apparent redeeming feature being that he could bake a decent cake. Son Gary's favourite pastime was goading next-door neighbour David Platt over his then girlfriend, Tina. David exacted revenge by tricking him into burgling Audrey Roberts' house, but on his release from prison, Gary finally showed signs of wanting to make something of his life by joining the army. At last there was one member of the family of whom Anna could be proud.

Anna and Eddie became foster parents to teenager Faye Butler in early 2011. But after the death of Faye's biological mum Jenny from a heroin overdose, Anna decided she wanted to officially adopt Faye. But Eddie disagreed, since the sulky girl was a whole lot of trouble. But when Eddie pushed Anna to choose between him or Faye, she chose her newly adopted daughter and the Windass marriage ended, with Eddie leaving and going to Germany.

Anna certainly had her hands full with Faye, who at the age of 13 unexpectedly gave birth to a baby girl, Miley, in the flat above the Corner Shop. And things got even more complicated when Faye's biological dad, Tim Metcalfe, moved in next door. Only in Weatherfield!

Anna found support from builder Owen Armstrong, whose daughter Izzy was dating

ABOVE: **She's Going Down! Murderous Tracy gets life in 2007** FAR LEFT: **Anna's relationship with Owen is pushed to breaking point by nasty Phelan in 2014** LEFT: **Anna and Eddie become foster parents to school girl Faye in 2011**

108

Anna's son Gary. But in 2014, Anna and Owen's relationship was put to the test by Owen and Gary's new builder boss, Pat Phelan. He began secretly flirting with Anna and then tried to force himself on her. When Anna told Gary what Pat had done, her angry ex-squaddie son attacked Pat with a plank of wood and left him for dead. However, Pat had CCTV footage of the attack and used it to blackmail Anna into sleeping with him.

Owen was disgusted when he found out what Anna had done, even though she'd been trying to help get Owen and Gary released from their crippling employment contract with Pat. Their relationship never quite recovered, and eventually Owen accepted a job offer in Aberdeen. Unfortunately for Anna, her nightmare with Pat Phelan was far from over, and he successfully framed her for pushing Faye's boyfriend off a ladder. She was sent to prison in 2017.

When the Nazir family moved into No. 6, it wasn't exactly home sweet home. Son Kal was killed when a fire broke out at nearby Victoria Court, and his mother Yasmeen discovered her husband Sharif had been having an affair with long-time family friend Sonia Rahman, and he was disowned by the family.

Kal's son Zeedan's own marriage to his sister Alya's university friend Rana Habeeb was doomed when Rana began a secret lesbian relationship with restaurant waitress Kate Connor. When the shock truth came out, Rana's strict parents Hassan and Saira tried to pay the couple to stay together for appearances' sake. Ultimately it was all too much for Zeedan to be around Rana, and in 2018 he abandoned his new street food restaurant Speed Daal and left Weatherfield.

ABOVE: **In 2014 Gary lashes out at Phelan after his builder boss begins harassing Anna**
RIGHT: **Married woman Rana begins a secret lesbian affair with Bistro waitress Kate in 2017**

RIGHT AND OPPOSITE: **In 2005, Katy Harris leaves a suicide note confessing to the murder of her dad Tommy, who she hit over the head with a wrench after discovering he lied about her boyfriend Martin cheating on her.**

I'm writing this to set the record straight once and for all, about what really happened the night my dad died. I couldn't get it into his head how much he'd hurt me tricking me into the abortion. All he could do was laugh and say it was better than winning the lottery. He kept gloating how he'd got his way and kept calling Martin a pervert, and I was getting madder and madder til finally I snapped and went out of control and hit him on the head with a wrench.

It didn't sink in rightaway, what I'd done then my mum came in. I thought I'd just hurt him a bit but when she held him in her arms and started to cry I realised he was dead. This is why the police found her DNA in his blood. I completely lost it and mum had to calm me down. We argued for ages about what to do. She said Dad would have died a hundred times before he'd see me go to prison, and in the end we decided not to tell anyone. We wiped our fingerprints off everywhere and went home and washed our clothes to get rid of my dad's blood

When mum was arrested I begged her to tell the truth but she wouldn't. I hated myself ever since and cannot live with what I'ce done especially as mum is in prison for it. I hope after reading this the police will release her IMMEDIATELY! I also hope my death will help pay for what I've done.

Katy Harris.

P.S please tell craig — I'M SORRY, for everything. If I could turn back the clock I would. ~~But that's impossible~~ But I can't. ~~I can't live with myself~~ ~~anymore~~. I don't deserve to live, anymore and death is the only way out for me.

RIGHT: **In 2005, a few weeks after the death of Angela Harris's husband Tommy at the hands of an "intruder", factory worker Hayley Cropper is suspicious when she catches Angela using the factory computer to print out this ominous warning.**

YOU'RE NEXT

Forever + Always in my heart

Missing You So much it hurts.

My darling Des.

Natalie. X

EK

LEFT: **Just a few weeks after marrying Rovers landlady Natalie Horrocks in 1998, bookie Des Barnes dies after being attacked by a gang of drug dealers in the living room at No.6.**

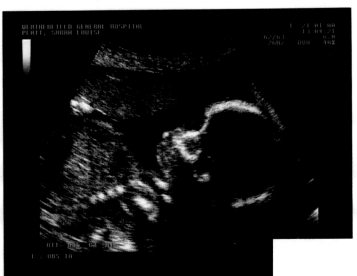

LEFT: **Sarah Platt's baby scan. Just after her 13th birthday in 2000, Sarah discovers she is pregnant by school classmate Neil Fearns. She gives birth to baby daughter Bethany in June 2000.**

113

Mums Name: *Sarah Platt.*

Weatherfield General Hospital
Anti-natal Clinic & Maternity Unit

Breaking hearts in a broken home

Gail Potter very nearly left the Street just as quickly as she'd arrived. In 1974, only months after settling into her job as a factory clerk, girl-about-town Gail got itchy feet. Then came her escape route – an interview to be an air stewardess. By the time she got through to the second round of interviews she was practically packing her suitcase right there and then. Who wanted to be working in a

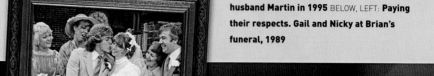

BELOW: **Marriage gloom for Gail and toy-boy husband Martin in 1995** BELOW, LEFT: **Paying their respects. Gail and Nicky at Brian's funeral, 1989**

№ 8 CORONATION ST.

RESIDENTS

1991–PRESENT
GAIL & DAVID PLATT

1991–1998, 2010–2012
NICK TILSLEY

1991–2000
MARTIN PLATT

1991–2007, 2015–2018
SARAH PLATT

2000–2007, 2015–2018
BETHANY PLATT

2002–2003
RICHARD HILLMAN

2008–2009
TINA MCINTYRE

2009–2010
JOE MCINTYRE

2011–2016
KYLIE PLATT

2011–PRESENT
MAX TURNER

2013–PRESENT
LILY PLATT

2014–2015, 2016
MICHAEL RODWELL

2016–2018
HARRY PLATT

2017–PRESENT
SHONA RAMSEY

washer Martin Platt was thinking of Gail as more than just a friend. However, with a ten-year age gap it took the loved-up twenty-something a long time to convince Gail that he was serious about her. But he managed it and on Christmas Day 1990, their son David was born. They married the following year and one of the Street's new houses, No.8, became the Platt family home.

Family life plodded along – David got a rabbit, Martin trained to be a nurse and Gail continued to fry bacon at the cafe. Until, much to her parents' horror, Sarah, aged 13, discovered she was pregnant and Bethany was born in 2000. Not that Martin could comment on Sarah's morals, seeing as he'd been having an affair with a fellow nurse for the last six months. His cheating wrecked their marriage, and Gail didn't take well to being on the receiving end of the infidelity for once. She despaired of ever finding another decent man.

It's often said that people find love in the most unexpected places, and so it was at Alma's funeral that Gail met her third husband, financial advisor Richard Hillman. Attentive, generous and family-minded, Richard seemed the perfect gentleman, and he put a smile on Gail's face for the first time in years.

He treated her to a luxury break in the Algarve, followed by a trip to Canada to see Nick, who was now living there. He even bought the whole family

factory when you could be sipping Campari with a pilot in Benidorm instead? But to her huge disappointment, Gail didn't get the job, and she's been in Weatherfield ever since.

With a life of foreign travel no longer an option, Gail took a fancy to the local heartthrob, mechanic Brian Tilsley instead, and, after weeks of flirting, a drunken Brian finally plucked up the courage to ask her out on a date. Much to his miserable mother Ivy's dismay, Gail married Brian in 1979, and they honeymooned on the Isle of Man. But the young couple's marriage wasn't to last and they divorced, mostly thanks to Gail's affair with Brian's cousin. They remarried in 1988, mainly for their children Sarah Lou and Nicky's sakes, and this time around, older and wiser, it looked like they were going to make a go of it – until Brian was stabbed to death outside a nightclub.

After Brian's death, Gail threw herself into work at Jim's Cafe on Rosamund Street, and it soon became clear that the Greasy Spoon's pot

LEFT: **Gail falling in love again, this time with pot washer Martin in 1989** BOTTOM: **Teenage Sarah is shocked to find out she is pregnant in 2000** BELOW, RIGHT: **Martin enjoys the bedside manner of fellow nurse Rebecca Hopkins in 1999**

I think I might watch the Queen's Speech, see if she's had a worse year than us...

SARAH

LEFT: **Gail doesn't approve of golden boy Nick and Leanne** BELOW, LEFT: **Audrey begins to worry she is losing her mind** BELOW, RIGHT: **Sarah adapts to life as a young mum**

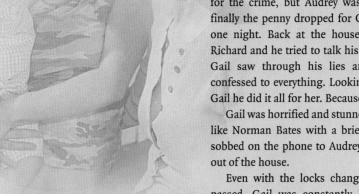

a brand-new people carrier and it was smiles all round. It looked like unlucky-in-love Gail had finally met Mr Right. But when it came to Richard Hillman, all was not as it seemed. The first clue to his sinister nature came when his business partner, Duggie Ferguson, fell to his death on a building site, and Richard robbed the safe rather than calling an ambulance

Mother-in-law Audrey wasn't as convinced by Richard as her daughter – there was something about him she just didn't trust. Meanwhile, Richard was very keen to get married, especially when he found out Gail would inherit £250,000 from Audrey's will. After the no-expense-spared wedding, Gail happily planned their comfortable future together, blissfully unaware that she didn't really know the man she had married at all.

Richard then upgraded his villainous credentials to murder by killing his ex-wife Patricia with a shovel. When he found himself facing bankruptcy, he tried to convince Gail that Audrey was going insane to get his hands on her money.

He even let himself into Audrey's house, took the batteries out of the smoke alarm and turned the hob on under the pan of milk, placing tea towels next to the gas ring to start a fire. As the tea towels began to smoulder, he quietly left the house.

Luckily, however, Steve McDonald and Archie Shuttleworth saw the flames and managed to drag Audrey out. Gail was relieved her mum was unharmed, but Richard was understandably less pleased. It was becoming clear this man was unhinged. Richard's next target was elderly investor Emily Bishop – but he ended up having to kill Maxine Peacock instead when she caught him trying to murder Emily whilst she was babysitting at No 4.

Richard framed tearaway teen Aidan Critchley for the crime, but Audrey was on to him, and finally the penny dropped for Gail in the Rovers one night. Back at the house, she confronted Richard and he tried to talk his way out of it, but Gail saw through his lies and eventually he confessed to everything. Looking crazed, he told Gail he did it all for her. Because he loved her.

Gail was horrified and stunned, saying, 'You're like Norman Bates with a briefcase.' While she sobbed on the phone to Audrey, Richard slipped out of the house.

Even with the locks changed, as the weeks passed, Gail was constantly looking over her

shoulder now that Richard was on the run. She was startled to arrive home one evening to find Richard waiting – smiling lovingly at her.

He then placed a letter on the sideboard saying it explained everything, before calmly leading her out to the garage where, to her horror, she saw he'd bound and gagged the children and strapped them in the car. He forced Gail into the passenger seat and tied her up, too. Richard then wound up the car windows and started the engine, and the sick reality finally sunk in for Gail – he was going to gas them all.

To her relief, she heard Audrey banging on the garage door, but as Tommy Harris and Kevin Webster broke the door open, Richard drove at full, tyre-screeching speed out of the garage.

He proved his madness by driving them to the Weatherfield Quays, where he plunged the car into the water to a chorus of gut-wrenching screams from his passengers. Miraculously, the whole family reappeared in the water one by one, gasping for air, unscathed. Richard Hillman was the only person to resurface as a corpse.

If Gail thought she'd made bad choices before when it came to men, then nothing compared to this. Standing on the quayside, trembling with shock, Gail took off her wedding ring and threw it into the canal. She didn't want to keep anything that would ever remind her of Richard Hillman.

But perhaps the family member affected most deeply by this terrifying experience was David, who has never been the same since. For Gail, this was the only way she could explain her son's subsequent evil behaviour. This included playing truant from school and sending eerie greetings cards to his mother, supposedly from Richard Hillman, ruining her new relationship with reflexologist Phil Nail. He then started a hate campaign against Charlie Stubbs, which resulted in David being nearly drowned in the bathtub by the psycho builder. Next he blackmailed Tracy Barlow, before happily committing perjury at her murder trial.

He nearly killed his niece, Bethany, when she swallowed an ecstasy pill he'd hidden in her doll. He also hospitalised brother-in-law-to-be, Jason Grimshaw, when he carefully loosened a piece of scaffolding at the builder's yard.

David's next plot was to ruin Sarah and Jason's big day – which he did by driving his car into the canal at the exact same spot chosen four years earlier by his loony stepfather. In 2008, he pushed his mum down the stairs in a frenzy when he found out she'd advised his feisty girlfriend, Tina, to have an abortion without telling him. A month later, perhaps not surprisingly, David had a major breakdown. He took a pole and attempted to smash up the street, before assaulting a policeman. Much to Gail's dismay, he was sent to jail for a month.

For a while, Tina was the only good thing in David's life, but eventually she tired of his malevolent scheming and moved out. Her father Joe was a kitchen fitter, and the prospect of a new set of units for No.8 was enough for Gail to start dating him. What she didn't know at the time was that he was also heavily in debt, a compulsive liar and had a history of depression. Gail certainly knew how to pick them.

Forced out of his flat, he willingly agreed to move in with her. Dreamily in love again, she chose to ignore his sudden flashes of temper and other irrational character traits that would have encouraged most women to send him packing. After injuring his back during one of his increasingly rare spells of work, he became addicted to painkillers and ended up trashing the medical centre, where Gail worked, in search of supplies. Still she forgave him. If her love for him wasn't quite blind, it was seriously in need of an eye test.

Desperate to keep his mounting debts a secret from Gail, he borrowed money from a loan shark. The loan was passed on to debt collector Rick

> **I've done all this for you, Gail. I've killed for you, that's how much I love you! Did Brian or Martin ever love you that much?**
>
> **RICHARD HILLMAN**

117

ABOVE, LEFT: **In shock, but still alive. The family's nightmare is finally over** RIGHT: **David endangers Bethany's life** RIGHT: **David goes on a rampage**

Neelan who not only doubled the repayments, but threatened both Joe and Tina with violence. Nevertheless, Joe bought an old boat, which he renovated and named Gail Force. With the boat parked outside No.8, he climbed aboard and proposed to Gail. To the despair of David and Audrey, who had long harboured grave reservations about Joe, she readily accepted.

Finally admitting that he owed thousands of pounds, Joe persuaded Gail to sell the house and move into a flat. To pay for the honeymoon, he borrowed from Ted Page, Gail's gay father (who had recently come into her life), but when the house sale fell through, Joe's financial crisis reached breaking point.

Hounded by Neelan, Joe escaped by whisking Gail off to the Lake District. There, her hopes of a romantic break were shattered when he revealed an elaborate plan: to fake his own death on the boat as part of an insurance scam. He didn't want to be parted from her, but it was the only solution he could see. Thus Gail was left sobbing inconsolably on the jetty as her husband of less than a month disappeared into the night. True to form, Joe couldn't even fake his death properly, accidentally falling into the water and drowning.

Gail was once, twice, three times a widow. The difference this time was that, by initially covering Joe's tracks, she would be accused of murder and temporarily sent to prison. But despite a false testimony from scheming neighbour Tracy Barlow, Gail was found not guilty at trial.

Having had her own brush with the law, it was perhaps fitting that Gail next fell for a criminal, Michael Rodwell. She caught Michael trying to burgle No.8, and when Michael was sent to prison, Gail paid him a visit. Gail took pity on Michael and began to help him get his life back on track when he was released. Michael became Gail's fifth husband in April 2015, but the following year, tragedy struck when Michael collapsed and died from a heart attack while trying to expose crooked local builder Pat Phelan. Gail later scattered Michael's ashes at the scenic spot where the couple were planning to renew their wedding vows.

But as well as her own tragic relationships, Gail has had to deal with the emotional fallout from her children's disastrous love lives. Eldest son Nick had a one-night stand with younger brother David's wife Kylie at Christmas in 2012. And when Kylie discovered she was pregnant, she was unsure if David or Nick was the father.

Learning of his wife and brother's betrayal, David launched a secret campaign of revenge, which culminated in Nick sustaining brain damage in a van smash. Kylie gave birth to a daughter, Lily, and a DNA test confirmed that David was indeed her father, but his deplorable behaviour towards Nick resulted in his banishment from the family for a while.

In 2015, Sarah Platt returned to Weatherfield with her now-teenage daughter Bethany, after living in Milan for seven years. Sarah made the

ABOVE: **Gail's family find themselves in the media spotlight when she stands trial, accused of Joe's murder** LEFT: **Gail marries Joe in 2010 but the marriage ends in tragic circumstances...**

mistake of falling for Kylie's drug-dealing ex, Callum Logan, who was fighting Kylie for custody of their son Max and already had an ongoing feud with David. But by the time Sarah saw Callum's true colours, it was too late. When he physically attacked Sarah at No.8, Kylie raced to her rescue and killed Callum by hitting him over the head with a wrench. For months, only David, Kylie and Sarah knew Callum's body was buried beneath the new garage annexe. Sarah later gave birth to Callum's son, Harry, but her murderous ordeal had all been too much, and she was eventually admitted to a psychiatric unit for help.

Tragedy struck hard at the heart of the Platt family when Kylie was fatally stabbed by Clayton Hibbs, a thug who had vowed revenge after his mate Callum's body was discovered buried at No.8. Kylie died on the cobbles in David's arms. Her death set off a terrible chain of events, as David turned vigilante to punish Kylie's killer himself, embarking on a suicidal mission to blow up Clayton's prison van en route to court. When he only narrowly avoided running over his daughter, David came to his senses and allowed Clayton to be served justice via a lengthy prison sentence.

Meanwhile, feeling misunderstood by her family, Bethany got mixed up with older man Nathan Curtis, who was secretly grooming her for an underage child sex ring. Bethany was flattered by the attention Nathan gave her and didn't realise something sinister was going on until Nathan pimped her out at a party to some of his mates, including crooked copper Neil Clifton. After attempting to go on the run and flee the police, Nathan, Neil and the rest of the grooming gang were found guilty in court and sent to prison in October 2017.

David's latest love interest, Shona Ramsey, has stayed the course despite an apparently insurmountable obstacle – that she's Clayton's estranged mother, a fact she initially kept secret from volatile David. But Shona proved her mettle by supporting Bethany, and she and David went on to forge a robust relationship, which turned out to be a godsend when David faced his darkest hour to date. In March 2018, David was drugged and raped by his new friend, mechanic Josh Tucker. Unable to speak about the traumatic event to anyone, David suffered in silence, even contemplating ending his life, before he finally summoned the strength to confide in Shona. Shona proved wonderfully supportive as David spoke to the police and his family about his ordeal, and as he begins to emerge from the pits of his despair, it looks like they could turn out to be one of the strongest couples ever to reside at No.8. Until the next catastrophe strikes, anyway.

119

11th March 2003.

To whom It may concern,

By the time you read this we will all be far from here. In this letter I want to explain everything and exonerate my dear wife Gail from any blame or suspicion.

Duggie Ferguson's death was an accident, he fell. I panicked. I desperatley needed money, so I robbed him. That was that.

But then my ex-wife Patricia started sticking her nose in and I couldn't put up with her causing trouble. I tried to explain to her how much I loved my family, but she wouldn't listen, she made threats, said bad things about Gail. And I snapped. I didn't want to kill her, I didn't MEAN to kill her.

If that shovel hadn't been there she'd still be alive. And so would my marriage. Because if I hadn't done that awful thing I could have clawed my way out, made everything good.

But what happened to Patricia sent me on this downward spiral, ending with the death of Maxine Peacock. I hate myself for that, for killing a beautiful young woman, for making her little kid grow up without his mum.

These are not the words of a madman, they're the words of a loving husband and father. I did what I did out of love. I hear you asking what kind of love is it that drives a man to try to kill his wife's mum? It's the kind of man who loves his wife enough to do it.

Don't think I wouldn't do anything to turn the clock back. Don't think I don't want to go back and say sorry to Audrey, Ashley, Gail, Sarah, young David and little Bethany for putting them all through hell. I'm not asking forgiveness, I know I'm a guilty man deserving punishment.

The one thing that kept me going when I was on the run was the hope I could turn my nightmares into dreams of us being together again - And while I can't profess to be a religious man I know we WILL now be back together again in heaven.

Yours truly,

Richard Hillman.

Victoria Court

Victoria Court

RESIDENTS

2008–2010
DEV ALAHAN

2008–2009
AMBER KALIRAI

2009
LUKE STRONG

2010
SUNITA, AADI & ASHA ALAHAN

2010
NATASHA BLAKEMAN

2010–2011
TINA MCINTYRE & GRAEME PROCTOR

2012–2017
NICK TILSLEY

2012–2014, 2016–2017
LEANNE BATTERSBY

2012–2013, 2016–2017
SIMON BARLOW

2013–2014
ROB DONOVAN

2014–2016
CARLA CONNOR

2015–2016, 2018–PRESENT
SARAH & BETHANY PLATT

2016–2017
TOYAH BATTERSBY

2016–PRESENT
ROBERT PRESTON

2017–PRESENT
MICHELLE CONNOR

2017
OLIVER BATTERSBY

2018–PRESENT
HARRY PLATT

2018–PRESENT
GARY WINDASS

2016–2018
JOHNNY & JENNY CONNOR

For those whose budget won't stretch to a traditional two-up two-down on Coronation Street, or just prefer a more modern living space, just around the corner is Victoria Court, a block of luxury apartments, which has seen a revolving door of residents come and go over the years.

In May 2015, the apartment building almost burned to the ground when Tracy Barlow broke into apartment No.12, intending to get even with her hated rival Carla for wrecking her takeover bid for the Rovers. Unaware her own daughter Amy was staying with Carla for the night, Tracy left a candle burning which started a fire. Leanne Battersby's fiancé Kal Nazir and Sophie Webster's girlfriend Maddie Heath were both killed in the crossfire when the building exploded. Thinking she was responsible for the blaze, Carla turned to booze and considered suicide in the aftermath. But just as the she was about to take a plunge off a cliff, guilty Tracy confessed to the crime, leading to her arrest.

There was more drama for Leanne when she was forced to give birth to her son, Oliver Battersby, while trapped in the lift at Victoria Court during a power cut in February 2017. She was stuck with stepsister Toyah, who followed instructions from nurse Rana Nazir outside the lift doors to deliver the baby. But Oliver's birth was surrounded by scandal, since the baby's biological dad was not Leanne's partner Nick but Rovers

> **Blokes are a total waste of space.**
>
> **GEMMA WINTER**

ABOVE: **Liz comforts grieving Johnny in the aftermath of his son Aidan's suicide in 2018**
BELOW: **Pregnant Leanne goes into labour whilst stuck in the lift with sister Toyah in 2017**

landlord Steve McDonald, following a one-night stand. The shock revelation would cost Steve his marriage to Michelle, and he lost the Rovers during the divorce settlement.

And tragedy struck for the Connor family in May 2018. Just as Johnny and his wife Jenny's bags were packed ready to start a new life in sunny Spain, Johnny's son Aidan committed suicide at his flat around the corner in Victoria Street. Caught in the middle of a family fight over who should rightfully inherit the factory from Aidan, grieving Johnny began to push Jenny away, accusing her of hating his beloved son, and sought comfort in the arms of Liz McDonald. This sort of behaviour never stays secret in Weatherfield, and as the Connors took the reigns of the Rovers Return, Liz's presence on the payroll meant it was only a matter of time before Jenny discovered her husband's betrayal. If they can weather the inevitable storm and stick together remains to be seen.

ABOVE: **Businessman Tony Gordon brings luxury living to the cobbles with the Victoria Court apartment complex**
FAR LEFT: **Carla's suspicions were confirmed when her brother Rob admits he murdered Tina**
LEFT: **During a clifftop confrontation with Carla in 2015, Tracy finally reveals what really happened the night of the fire...**

The Viaduct Bistro

It's a wonder the Bistro is still open for business after all the shock events that have happened on the site of the restaurant over the years. If No.13 has a reputation as the unluckiest house on the Street, the business premises beneath the railway viaduct, where the Bistro first opened in 2011, must come a close second.

In 1967, a goods train derailed and crashed onto the Street trapping residents, including battleaxe Ena Sharples. Thirty years later, deranged ex-cabbie Don Brennan met his maker when he failed to run over enemy Mike Baldwin, drove his car into the viaduct wall and the vehicle exploded. Then in 2010, a gas explosion at the newly opened The Joinery bar caused the infamous tram derailment and the deaths of residents Molly Dobbs and Ashley Peacock.

But that didn't stop Nick Tilsley from opening Nick's Bistro on the very same spot, hopefully with a good insurance policy! The rota of staff and the restaurant name have changed over the years, but not the series of unfortunate events that have occurred within its walls...

ABOVE: **In 2016, Gail and Nick lock David in the cellar to stop him avenging Kylie's death** BELOW: **Tracy is an uninvited guest at Nick and Carla's wedding in 2016**

The restaurant hosted its first wedding in 2015 when Sally Webster and Tim Metcalfe tied the knot. But the ceremony was thrown into doubt when Tim called off the nuptials upon discovering that Sally had kissed her ex, Kevin, some months earlier. Sally begged Tim's forgiveness and insisted she would be waiting at the appointed hour in her wedding outfit, ready to marry him. With the clock ticking, Sally's confidence that Tim would back down was beginning to wane until he finally burst through the doors and made an honest woman of her.

In 2016, Nick's own wedding to Carla Connor fell apart when the bride confessed to a fling with his chef, Robert Preston. Nick's devoted mum Gail dealt Carla an almighty slap across the face. The following year, during a family celebration, Michelle Connor was devastated when her hubby Steve admitted that he was the father of Leanne Battersby's newborn baby, Oliver, following a one-night stand. The discovery came just a month after Michelle and Steve's own baby son, Ruairi, was born prematurely and died upon delivery in hospital.

124

The Viaduct Bistro

PROPRIETORS

2011–2017
NICK TILSLEY

2016–PRESENT
ROBERT PRESTON

2017–PRESENT
MICHELLE CONNOR

> **I win.**

ANNA'S FINAL WORDS TO SERIAL KILLER PAT PHELAN

RIGHT: **Chaos on the cobbles when a tram derails and crashes onto the Street**
BELOW: **Anna Windass kills Phelan during their final showdown** BOTTOM: **Kirk, Jason and Ciaran bravely rescue a survivor from the burning wreckage**

The Bistro has been a crime scene on several occasions, so there's always been plenty of scandalous news for the *Weatherfield Gazette* to report. But it's always wise for the management to say, 'No comment!', if they want restaurant customers to keep on coming back. Finding out your posh burger and chips were cooked in the same kitchen where infamous serial killer Pat Phelan was stabbed to death by Anna Windass would probably be enough to put anyone off their food!

Audrey's Hair and Beauty Salon

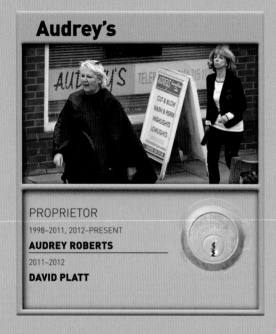

Audrey's

PROPRIETOR

1998–2011, 2012–PRESENT
AUDREY ROBERTS

2011–2012
DAVID PLATT

In September 2016, Audrey's was nominated as Best Small Salon in the Greater Manchester Stylist Awards. The judges must have been unaware of the various hair-raising happenings at 2 Coronation Street since Audrey Roberts took over the business from Fiona Middleton when she left Weatherfield in 1998.

In 2008, Audrey's grandson David Platt went on an angry rampage around the Street and smashed the salon windows, interrupting Rita Sullivan mid hair-do. Pensioner Edna Hargreaves passed away under the drier in 2011, just moments after complimenting David's hair-washing skills. He's good with his hands, is David. And then there have been unwanted visits from thugs, Audrey collapsing from a heart attack, and her daughter Gail storming into the salon to throw bottles of shampoo and conditioner at her love-cheat neighbour Eileen Grimshaw, causing a catfight which spilled out onto the Street!

BELOW: **Ken and Audrey share an intimate moment after he finds her collapsed at the salon in 2016**
RIGHT: **Family feud. David refuses to sign back ownership of the salon to Audrey in 2012**

Over the years the salon has changed names a few times. There have been squabbles over ownership, and Audrey almost cashed in the business to go on a world cruise with handsome male escort Lewis Archer, who turned out to be a con man and attempted to woo most of the women in Weatherfield. But at its heart, Audrey's has always been a family business with David and his wife Kylie, Sarah Platt and her daughter Bethany all having worked there – and bringing their fair share of drama to daily life at the salon. It's no wonder the lady needs a G&T or two across the road at the Rovers once the day's work is done.

"**D'you know, I reckon there's a great big poster of you on the wall in the local loony bin, with your mobile number underneath.**"

AUDREY ROBERTS
TO GAIL PLATT